WHEN THE SHEEP BITE

Loving The Church Even When It Hurts

Jason R. Velotta

For more information, sermons, bible studies, and apologetic material, contact: www.jasonvelotta.com
Edited by Valerie Hupp and Cheri Velotta

Original and modified cover art by JR Foto and CoverDesignStudio.com

ISBN: 9781522966623

First Edition: 2016

For Dana, Jacob, Jesse, and Sophie:
Jesus' bride is sometimes hard to deal with, but she is worth it.

"I have been hurt deeply by people in the Church; brothers in Christ I considered dear friends who betrayed my trust. That hurt does not stop just because I see a meme, as Jason writes, "with pictures of puppies and children." Learning to love the very person who caused our hurt is difficult, and Jason Velotta's book gives us hope, that in the midst of pain, we can still love...even when the sheep bite."

- Dr. J.R. Miller, Dean of Online Learning and Professor at Southern California Seminary.

Wherever two or more gather sin, hurts, wounds and problems are bound to appear! What do we do and how do we make it? What about personal choices and the response of those that hurt us? *When the Sheep Bite* is a clarion call for every believer to view all of life through the lens of the life-changing Gospel.

Jason Velotta has penned an insightful, clear, often humorous and powerful answer to one of the biggest problems in the Church - how to survive sheep bites! The Church is populated with sinners who are frequently flesh-dominated and sometimes very hurtful. This is true, but the answer is the Glorious Gospel of Jesus Christ, and Jason repeatedly calls the Bride back to the Rock.

While the questions are many and each situation is varied, the answer remains constant - The Gospel. We forgive because we are forgiven and we love because we are loved. Life hurts, and even good, godly people sin, but the truth shared in *When the Sheep Bite* will set you free, if you let it. Choose wisely, the Church needs you to do so!

Dr. Jeff Klick
Senior Pastor, Hope Family Fellowship, Kansas City, KS
Instructor - The Institute for Church Management

Contents

Introduction

D o you know someone who is hard to love? Have you ever been emotionally hurt by another person? Dumb questions...I know. Someone's face already popped into your mind, didn't it? We all have "that person" in our lives. You know who it is. Everyone chooses to love them from afar, which usually means, "Stay away from them." Maybe you forgave them long ago, but every now and again those feelings of bitterness resurface. It's hard to love the people who have hurt us! But what happens if it's a member of your church? If you are a Christian, you know the struggle. Jesus told us to love one another...but surely Jesus makes exceptions for people like Mrs. Busybody over there...right?

New Flash: even in church sometimes people can be hard to love. Shocking...I know. Church should be the one place where we feel safe...shouldn't it? Regardless of what many think, the church is not filled with perfectly Holy people.[1] It is made up of wretched sinners who have been saved and transformed by grace. Let's not beat around the bush. We just waste time when we try to ease into the subject of unloveable people with flowery words and lots of compliments.

Jesus commanded us to love the brethren even when they're hard to love. You know it and I know it. Some church people are hard to love and honestly, sometimes you and I *are too*! This book is about loving those who have hurt us and making sure we ourselves are not hurting others. Yet, before we dive into the problem and discover the solution, I need to make a few things perfectly clear.

First, this is not an outlet for venting frustrations about mean people. We won't be excessively dwelling on cases when people have hurt or offended us. That solves nothing. Most likely, you already have a laundry list of ways people have hurt you. I do understand the occasional need to vent, but that is not our focus here. We all know that people can be unkind. Producing a catalog of how unloving others have been is just beating a dead horse. Going over our hurts again and again only stirs up the same old thoughts of bitterness and resentment. That is exactly what we don't want. The point of this book is to understand what it means to love them…biblically.

Second, we will not engage in "church bashing."

---

[1] Believers are perfect in the Father's sight through the sacrifice of Jesus, but not perfected in our thoughts and deeds yet.

Unfortunately, there are already lots of books like that. Although the church is composed of sinners, which means church people are certainly capable of sinning against us, she is still the perfect bride of Jesus. If you desire to be justified in neglecting the church because she has been mean to you, this book isn't for you. God has set His redemptive love on the body of Christ and, despite how we may have been injured by her, she is absolutely perfect in His sight. Jesus bought and paid for that perfect righteousness with His own blood. So, we tread on very dangerous ground if we go after her with tooth and claw. Our purpose is to love the people God loves, even if it is extremely difficult.

Third, we won't be clobbering the congregation for the way they treat the pastor. Once again, that has been done. Of course, pastors do get hurt a lot. But everyone who invests themselves in the lives of people gets hurt. Today, many people see an unbiblical distinction between the pulpit and the pew. The pastor isn't the only individual called to disciple believers, evangelize, and edify the brethren. Every Christian is commanded to do these things. Therefore, our focus will be on any believer who is disappointed and hurting because of bad experiences with the church. We won't be exploring this topic specifically from a shepherd's point of view.

Fourth, this book is not entitled, *How To Be A Doormat*. We are learning how to love the unloveable. We are not learning how to lie down and let people walk all over us. Scripture commands believers to separate from people under certain circumstances. We will discover where we draw that line. Loving the brethren doesn't mean being a punching bag for others.

Fifth, I will not be condescending at all. We are all in the same boat here. Both you and I have been hurt by others, but let's be honest right from the start. Both you and I have injured other people too. At times in this book, I will speak of people who are unloveable and disagreeable. While I may not explicitly state the fact at every point, we have all been in this category at times. Loving church people is not an "us-versus-them" conflict. I can be just as offensive and ill tempered as any other church member, and I often am! Can I get an amen?[2]

We are learning how to love Jesus' people even when it hurts. Christ commands us to love those who are difficult to love. But before we start the journey, we must cast away the idea that our conduct among the brethren has always been flawless. There is no room for condemnation when we have all been guilty at one time or another.

"A new commandment I give to you, that you love one another, even as I have loved you, that you also love one another. By this all men will know that you are My disciples, if you have love for one another." – John 13:34-35

---

[2] Those who know me are nodding their heads in approval.

Chapter 1

Another "Love" Book?

I know what you're thinking. "Great...another book telling me how to love people." I thought the exact same thing when I sat down to write this book. To be honest, I think Christians have enough "fluffy" books presenting love as a warm and fuzzy emotion. Love is often seen as the magical element that makes life worth living. Love causes all life to break forth with blossoming flowers, sweet songs, unicorns, and colorful rainbows. Love just happens in our hearts. It takes over and all of life falls under its spell. I can only speak for myself, but I don't have any use for books like that. Obviously, there is a great market for them. Throw a rock in a Christian bookstore and you will probably hit one. And they all say the same thing. Just pour out your heart and feel the warmth of this indescribable emotion as it envelops you in a mystical cocoon of gooey goodness. Blah, blah, blah...

Teaching me about touchy-feely, saccharine infested love doesn't really help me walk through the actual heartaches and sufferings of this world. This sentimental love doesn't help me when people are mean, vindictive, and downright nasty. A "love" feeling in my heart doesn't help me when I am called to act out real love to those who are impossible to love (Luke 6:28). Disciples of Christ, living in the real world, are called to love all men, but specifically to love and invest themselves in "the brethren." Christians are commanded to lay down their very lives for each other as we serve one another in love. Sounds great doesn't it? But what happens when fellow believers don't reciprocate that love? What happens when loving the church means gulping down pride and putting faith into action?

"Oh," you say, "This is going to be one of those legalistic – *love people or else* - books." No, I don't have any use for those books either. But even now, I can hear the voice in my head saying, "you are commanded to love - so just do it!" But is that real love? Is true biblical love nothing more than a raw action motivated by a slogan Nike uses to promote athletic shoes?

So let's clear this up right at the beginning. This is a book about how broken sinners can be transformed by the gospel to truly love other broken sinners. Jesus loves His church, and the church is filled with sinners, forgiven by grace. No one in the church has reached the pinnacle of perfection yet.[3] We all know this. All of us are broken. Nevertheless, Jesus continually demonstrates love for His church. He loved her

---

[3] Present company included

so much that He took on flesh, lived a perfect life, and died on a cross so that His church could be redeemed. Even though His bride is often marred by sin, selfishness, and all manner of fleshly pursuits, He still stands in her place before the judgment bar of God's law. Of course, when believers sin God disciplines them, but His love for them is still the same. We are called to love the church like that. We are called to invest ourselves and share our lives in service to the brethren. Bearing one another's burdens is supposed to be the Christian's lifestyle. We are commanded to love and care for those whom Jesus loves and cares. But how do I do that when some of the "brethren" continually hurt me? I know the correct answer. You are supposed to love like Jesus loved...*unconditionally*. I know...I know. I get it. But my question is how? Give me the nuts and bolts of it. Does the Bible tell me how I keep my heart in check when pride or anger rises up in me, or when I feel wronged? Does Scripture give me the explanation of how this Christ-like love looks in real life? I don't need to be instructed on how to fake it. I'm pretty good at that already! I really want to love the people Jesus loves...I really do, but how much do I take before I draw the line? Is it even possible for my heart to love those who continually sin against me? On top of all that, what happens if I am the one who is treating others like dirt? How can I protect myself against myself? When someone hurts me, my knee-jerk reaction is to be resentful, angry, and prideful. When that happens, I usually become the hurtful brother. I want retribution when I am wronged. So, this book will address two main issues. How do I love when others aren't loveable? And how do I love in such a way that I don't become a person who is un-loveable?

In order to love the church like Jesus I need more than sentimental hallmark card sayings. I need more than clichés about the beauty of love and memes[4] with pictures of puppies and children in them. Loving people like Jesus commands is hard! It's heavy labor. I'll go out on a limb and say it's all but impossible! When things get downright nasty and people seem impossible to love, what do I do? When I get bombarded with stress and the burdens of life, how do I keep *myself* from being impossible to love? Anyone who has spent time in the church knows that trying to love people often hurts. People are wicked and rotten to the very core (that includes you and I.) The Bible announces this fact without apology (Rom. 3:10-18).

My natural heart is just as wicked as everyone else's. But as a believer, indwelt with the Spirit of God, the Bible says I received God's love in order to love others...even when they don't love me. More than that, we are all commanded to love people when they hate us. We are commanded to love them when they mistreat us and persecute us. Declaring that we must love unkind people makes great sentimental after-school movies, but if you have ever struggled with loving someone who seemed unloveable, you know that it's tough. No platitude about the value of love will help when all hell is breaking loose in your heart!

---

[4] If you don't know what a meme is, ask someone under thirty years old.

If I hear one more abstract cliché about love being the feeling that makes life worth living and brings a surreal happiness, I'll throw up. Please don't misunderstand me, I believe in biblical love, in fact, that's what this book is all about. True love for Christ and His church is real and available in the lives of believers. There is an answer to all these questions and I want them! I want to experience the love of Christ as well as having others experience the love of Christ through me. I really do love Jesus and I really do love Jesus' bride, the Church. But what exactly does this love look like? Is love nothing more than an emotion falling from the sky as it sweeps you off your feet in a windstorm of unbridled compassion and empathy? Does this love "take over" my heart and cause me to understand the stresses and issues that cause other people to act unkindly? We never really know the struggles other people have when they lash out, would this heart-felt love help work through all that? At this point I am sure of only one thing. True biblical love, the kind of love that Jesus commands, is hard work!

Failing to Love the Bride

If you are part of the body of Christ, I think you know exactly how difficult love can be. Church isn't a place where all the righteous people gather on Sunday. This may be what the world thinks of the church (and maybe what some churches think of themselves) but that's a misrepresentation of the Church. The local fellowship of believers is made up of wretched sinners still fighting against their sin. The only thing different about Christians is that they have been saved by the grace and mercy of God. By that grace through faith, these sinners have been born again and have been indwelt by God Himself. But there is still a problem. Even as saints of God, wholly justified in His sight, we continue to live in fleshly bodies. We still live in a fallen world. Our hearts are still deceitfully wicked (Jer. 16:9.) Make no mistake church member; someone in the church is going to hurt your feelings! Someone is going to rub you the wrong way…purposefully. If it hasn't happened yet, just wait…it's coming. Not only this, but you will also hurt someone else's feelings. Your stresses, your sins, and your flesh will inevitably use you as a vehicle to damage others. This is just a fact of life when serving along side other people. Look down your row Sunday morning. If you don't see someone that's hard to get along with…it's probably you!

Loving people who don't care about loving others or being loved is probably one of the biggest reasons people leave the church. Every believer is called to give sacrificially, serving the fellowship to which he or she belongs. When this task is taken seriously (as it should be by all believers) it always involves making sacrifices for others. Many times Christians sacrifice free time, family time, and even their own health to make sure they are available when people need them. Believers do that for one another. The love of God works through them. But what happens when the believer who has sacrificed so much needs something? What happens when church members do not reciprocate that sacrifice and care? Remember that even the most devout and caring believer is still a sinner at heart. More often than not, when this loving Christian's sacrificial love is not returned by the same people he served faithfully, the sinful flesh rises in him and he becomes resentful and bitter. It has definitely happened to me. That is the problem. What does biblical love look like when everything in our hearts is crying "foul?" How do you love people when you are always aware of the fact that they may turn on you at any minute? How do keep from becoming the kind of people who caused our bitterness in the first place? When others hurt us our natural reaction is to hurt them back. But then we become the very thing we despise in others.

Some people don't worry about these questions at all. Their idea of love is not biblical. They only know a superficial love. But we are called to love people like Christ loved. Yet, we often deceive ourselves into thinking we are keeping this command just because we are not presently holding any grudges. As we look into the biblical definition of love in this book, we will find that failing to love like Christ, more often than not, manifests itself as indifference rather than hatred. When we separate ourselves from the fellowship of the brethren because we feel wronged, we demonstrate how little we love like Christ. Maybe we don't get angry and lash out, but instead we disconnect from the fellowship. This is perhaps the most common type of loveless church member. The opposite of love is not hatred. The opposite of love is indifference and neglect. This lack of love is devastating both to the fellowship of believers and to the individual Christian.

But most importantly, failing to love people as Jesus commands hinders our relationship with God. Jesus said,

> "Therefore if you are presenting your offering at the altar, and there remember that your brother has something against you, leave your offering there before the altar and go; first be reconciled to your brother, and then come and present your offering" (Matt. 5:23-24).

Christ cannot speak more clearly here. Notice that it doesn't just say, "if you are angry with your brother." Jesus says, "If someone has something against you..." you should go be reconciled. Wait just a minute! All kinds of people may hold something against me! How am I responsible for that? Circumstances notwithstanding, the point of the passage is that your relationship with your "brothers"[5] affects your relationship with God. You may be caught up in a wonderful spirit of worship on Sunday morning, but Jesus says if you have unresolved issues with your brother, leave your gift (of worship) on the altar and be reconciled to your brother first. Then come and offer your sacrifice. Our relationship with fellow believers has a direct bearing on our relationship with God.

Those who have been born again by God's Spirit are your brothers and sisters. In one sense, all people are part of the human family because they are created in the image of

---

[5] "brothers" and "brethren" are consistently used in Scripture to speak of the family unity of the Christian Church.

God, but Christians are united in the family of God through Christ. Believers are adopted into a perfected family. Regardless of how mature (or immature) a Christian may be at this moment, Jesus valued them enough to give His life for them. In essence, when we neglect or forsake the brethren, we are trivializing the value of Christ's sacrifice! Then in turn, it doesn't take long before our own life becomes spiritually dry and joyless. Perhaps you have experienced this and not fully understood why it happens. Fellowship (true fellowship) with the brethren is an essential part of a believer's growth in Christ. God uses fellowship to grow us in the fruits of the Spirit. Galatians 5:22-23 tells us the Spirit produces love, joy, peace, patience, kindness, goodness, faithfulness, gentleness, and self-control. The Spirit not only produces these fruits in the life of the believer, but He continues to develop them throughout our lives. Fellowship with the brethren is an integral way He develops these fruits. How are we to grow in patience unless someone tests our patience? How are we to grow in gentleness or self-control unless others test the limits of our self-control and gentleness? Certainly there can be no growing relationship with God where there is no growing fellowship with Christ's bride. Is fellowship with Jesus' church easy? Absolutely not! Does fellowship with the church often involve conflict and contention? Of course it does, but that's the point. Just as iron sharpens iron, so one man sharpens another. Yet we often fail to realize that a piece of iron doesn't sharpen another peice unless you whack them together. Most of us are so enamored with our own comfort that we pull out of the fellowship when things get tough. Dealing with all the conflict is just too emotionally draining.

Conflict among the brethren also causes believers to move around from church to church, hoping to find that one congregation that will be filled with perfect, loving people. Unfortunately there is no such place this side of heaven. The body of Christ is not filled with perfect people so there aren't any perfect churches. Expecting sinners to exhibit perfect goodness in their relationships is not a reasonable demand. Many people have come to the church to be in the presence of good people, but it doesn't take long to realize that no one is good. The clarion cry of the offended church member is, "I would go to church, but I can't find one that isn't filled with a bunch of hypocrites." Of course the church is filled with hypocrites (you and I included.) McDonalds and Wal-Mart are filled with hypocrites too but we have no problem spending time there. "Why," you may ask? Because we have a hunger and thirst for what is at McDonalds. An offensive employee is not a good enough excuse to deter us from seeking nourishment. If only we could hunger and thirst after righteousness, an offensive church member would never keep us away from our spiritual nourishment.

Other people leave churches simply because the congregation or the pastor didn't give them enough attention. Hopefully we can all see how foolish this is. But we must admit that there are some people who have real problems that remove them from church. Sometimes, church people genuinely hurt others and the pain of this experience drives them away. They just aren't ready to love people they know are going to let them down again. These folks leave church all together. They refuse to even darken the door of any church building. Maybe they choose to have a "family" church in their home on Sunday. I'm all for church planting, but some people choose this option simply because they can't get along with other people. Dismissing these people as childish is all too easy, but setting aside the foolishness of leaving church because no one shook your hand, there are real issues that need to be addressed. Not everyone is being childish because they don't want to be hurt again. Some people have intense hurts and feelings of betrayal. How can they love someone who will inevitably fail them? How can we come to grips with the fact that we are all wicked...all of us?

How to love in the face of sin is the subject of this book. We know we are supposed to love unconditionally, but we just don't know how! As a believer, I can't just close my eyes and pretend. Going through the motions is just not good enough. As a follower of Christ, I don't want to act like I love people. I want to genuinely love people like Christ loves them. I want to love people in the face of the harshest treatment. When people are using me for their own purposes and slamming my name in the dirt, I want to respond with love. Showing Christ's love despite discouragement, doubt, and disappointment is something for which believers hunger. We just need to know how! We usually don't have a problem giving advice to someone else.

It's easy to tell others, "Just let it go."[6] Of course letting bitterness go is the right answer. We know what we are supposed to do.

Personally, I just have a problem actually doing it. I can temporarily force myself to forgive when people hurt me. By sheer force of will I can dismiss feelings of discouragement when someone stabs me in the back. But what do I do thirty minutes later when those feelings pop right back up? What do I do when every time I lay eyes on that person those feelings rise up again? Do I just swallow those feelings, smile, and try to be nice? Do I just keep on serving and fellowshipping even though there is enmity brewing in my soul?

This continuing cycle of being hurt by others, trying to love them, and having to repeatedly fight through the whole process is one reason why so many churches are seeing their numbers and involvement dwindle. I can attest to the fact that living this way is incredibly tiresome. It hurts when relationships go bad and church friendships get unpleasant. It hurts when we pour our lives into a fellowship of believers only to see many of them rise up against us because they disagree about the color of the carpet. These conflicts often drive us to become the kinds of people we decry and that damages us most of all. When we feel wronged we tend to focus only on ourselves. We seek to fulfill our own desires and protect our own well-being.

---

[6] As I break out singing the song from Disney's Frozen.

When we suffer from the maltreatment of others, we start thinking we deserve better things and in response, we usually start mistreating others to meet this end. This inward focus leads to our neglecting the service Jesus called us to perform. We end up becoming the very thing we are condemning in others.

Pictures of puppies and quaint inspirational quotes can't help you navigate through those waters. Pure emotional sentimentalism is useless in this battle. True love for Christ and His church has to be something much deeper. Love has to be something alive in us. Our feelings (even the deep feelings love often engenders) are simply not reliable. They ebb and flow depending on our circumstances. No moral quotations about love will lift us up when the weight of bitterness and resentment comes crashing through the roof of our lives. We simply can't put out that four-alarm fire with a water pistol. We need something greater. This deficit in us is common knowledge for Christ followers. But there seems to be a lack of understanding as to the nature of biblical love and how that love manifests in our lives.

However, because many in the body of Christ are overcome with Hollywood caricatures and marketing messages about the meaning and function of love, they are wholly unprepared to fight this battle when it arises in the church...and it always arises. What happens next is predictable.

Three Kinds of "Church Hurt" People

Church members respond in different ways when people in their fellowship hurt them. Some people with hurt feelings just quit. Emotionally investing in people is just too difficult for them. Usually, this group searches for an excuse to leave rather than admitting their unwillingness to remain invested in the fellowship. You will hear, "The church didn't meet my needs so I am not going back." True Christians may be led to move their membership to another fellowship, but abstaining from church altogether isn't an option for the true believer in Christ. The Spirit inside a believer will discipline him or her to desire fellowship with God's people. Disciples will definitely fellowship somewhere. Those who choose to "forget the whole thing" and fall back into their previous lifestyle, give evidence that they were never Christ's people (1 John 2:19).

Other people truly desire fellowship but are so disappointed and hurt, they are honestly afraid to open themselves up to that kind of pain again. They really do love God's church but they simply can't deal with the reality of clashing personalities and the inevitable pains of bearing other people's burdens. All these people want is a place where God's children love each other and it's safe to lay their lives on the line in service to each other. That is the ideal setting for the body of Christ but in a fallen world, that will never be perfectly realized. That kind of perfect church won't exist until we are glorified with Christ in eternity.

Leaving church isn't the only option when Christ's sheep bite. Many people still attend church but no longer invest themselves in the fellowship. In their minds, simply being present during the worship service fulfills the requirement of fellowship. Coming to church, worshiping God, and being instructed from God's word is enough for them. Being deeply involved in people's lives is just too painful. Bearing one another's burdens costs more than they are willing to pay. It hurts when people don't reciprocate the love they have been shown. For these hurting believers, fellowship only leads to pain. To be sure, if someone close to them is in need they will spring into action, but as far as being a principal part of the local assembly or investing their life into others' growth and discipleship...that is too risky. That kind of sacrifice gets in the way of their lives. These members are really just placeholders in the sanctuary pews. They refuse to be involved in the ministry or service of the church and they shy away from anywhere the congregation gathers outside of the scheduled services. But we must remember of whom we are speaking. We are not talking about heathens who hate others and don't want any part of the church. We are talking about people who threw themselves fully into loving the brethren and were deeply wounded by some of Christ's sheep. Because of their wounds, they inadvertently become the people who neglect and hurt others by their lack of love. In the final chapter of this book, we will see that neglecting the body is just as damaging as denying it (cf. Gal. 6:1-5). But these people are not distancing themselves because of their animus against the church. They distance themselves because they don't want to be hurt anymore. It's just too costly to be intimately involved in lives of other people.

But retreating into solitude is not the answer. This only stunts the spiritual growth of the separated believer. Christ collects His bride in fellowship in order to mature and grow them together. Where there is no fellowship and love among the brethren, there is no growth in the fruits of the Spirit, but we will have more to say about this later.

Finally, there is a third category of people dealing with this type of disappointment in God's people. They don't quit church and they don't retreat into isolation. Instead, these people remain faithful and continue giving of themselves. They experience the same pain and feel the deep discouragement when hurt, but they also have a deep and abiding love for Christ and His commandments. They are well aware of Jesus' command to love the brethren and feed His sheep. They also understand that Scripture tells us loving the brethren is a defining characteristic of believers. We will see this fact in Scripture cited throughout this book. These hurting believers continue to serve despite their pain.

Because they know Jesus' command to bear one another's burdens, when the resentment and bitterness sets in on this last category of believers, they fall into guilt, despair, and shame. Rather than hide on the back row of the church,[7] they beat themselves up knowing that Jesus has

---

[7] Disclaimer: Not all back row church members are hiding, but many "hiding" church members are on the back row. (Happy now Valerie?)

commanded them to do something they seem unable to do. This group feels defeated because their hearts don't seem capable of obeying the command to love. As soon as they fight off their bitterness, it seems like only a few moments pass before those same feelings resurface. They spend their days fighting to love people, some of whom couldn't care less. Inevitably, reoccurring feelings of resentment followed by shame drive these believers to feel they are inadequate to serve in Christ's church. This results in an unhealthy life of introspection as the focus of their efforts becomes "getting themselves right" instead of serving those whom Christ loves, and reaching a lost world.

Perhaps you can see yourself in one of these categories (or a mixture of them). I know I have. Together we will discover the true meaning of biblical love for both Christ and His church. If we are to love as Christ loves, we surely must love in the face of persecution, mistreatment, and abuse. Christ definitely showed this kind of love as He experienced all the hatred and malice of the world. He loved His disciples even when they abandoned Him at His greatest moment of need. If Scripture is authoritative and Jesus meant exactly what he said,[8] we can't just throw the baby out with the bathwater. We can't just say loving unloveable church people is too hard so I'll just give up trying. That's not an option. Yet, we also know that the popular caricature of love's sappy goodness isn't any help when dealing with

---

[8] It most certainly is and He most certainly did!

people in the trenches of God's Kingdom. So, what is the solution to all this? …I am glad you asked.

Problem…Solution?

Before we start outlining Scripture's answer for loving the unloveable, I need to make something perfectly clear. I am not writing this because I have mastered the art of loving unloveable people. In fact, many people would say that I myself am a church member who is extremely hard to love. I have not found the spiritual secret that allows me to forgive and forget without struggling through bitterness and resentment, nor have I found that fountain of goodness in myself that keeps me from mistreating others when I feel wronged. I'm not very good at loving people at all. I probably struggle more than most when it comes to forgiving those who have stabbed me in the back. I don't do well with those who have been presumptuous with my time while giving none of theirs. And it is this very flaw that causes me to exhibit the same offensive behavior I judge in others. My own bitterness causes me to withdraw my love and become the person who abuses another's love. "So," you may ask, "Why in the world do you think you should be writing a book on this subject?"

Once again, thank you for asking. I am writing this precisely because I have so much trouble with this issue. Because of my shortcomings and my own sin, I have found that loving selfish people is a struggle for me. It's not just a struggle. It's a sin. And this sin pushes me to become just like those I criticize. This proclivity in me is something that I should never accept and try to live with. I should never come to the conclusion that I am just "this way," and abandon the fight to love people. As a follower of Christ, I can't do that. Being unloving is something I desperately desire to overcome. I don't have an option because Christ commanded me to love the brethren.

But every time I turn around, my sinful heart rises up and brings all those feelings of hurt and discouragement back. How do I love the church the same way Jesus loves them? These same wretched, sinful, backstabbing, selfish, uncaring people (of which I am most certainly one) are the very people for whom God sent His Son. We are the same people that Jesus loved enough to give His life for. I want to be like Jesus and I know I should. I know I am just as sinful and wretched as everyone else (if not worse) and Jesus loves me too. I know I should love the church the same way He loves me…I know this. But my question is, "how?" How do I do it? Can I change the way I feel? Can I change the very impulses of my nature? There must be a way to accomplish this because Jesus commanded me to love them even when they hurt me.

I have read many books on Christ's love and loving other people, but I have not found one that biblically attempted to show me how. This is the question I hope to resolve by the end of this book. I could write another "love" book filled with platitudes and clichés, which demonstrates the central place love deserves in our walk with Christ. But that kind of book isn't going to help me, and I'd be willing to bet it isn't going to help you either. I already know how important love is and how much Christ loves His people. I want to know how to love when it hurts. I need to find out how to love the people that use me and throw me away when they don't need me anymore. I need to know how to love people who absolutely want to destroy me and I desperately need to know how to keep myself from becoming an abuser or neglector of the brethren. And please don't forget, I am talking about church people. I'm not talking about the rabid secular folks trying to stamp out every hint of Christianity. The biggest problems in the church today are the people in the church (and that includes me.) We can be spiteful, hurtful, and very...very selfish. As a pastor I am called to admonish people and teach right doctrine. As believers we are all called to confront sin and lovingly bring discipline to each other (Matt. 18:15-20). But we are also called to love each other, even when we aren't worth loving. Paul tells us we fulfill Christ's law of love when we bear one another's burdens (Galatians 6:2-3). We are called to love each other despite how bad we hurt one another. How do I do that? I'm good at faking it. Pretending is not a problem; in fact it's really easy. But I don't want to fake it. I want to genuinely love Christ's Church. How do I do that? Before we find the answer to that question, we need to define the biblical reality of love toward the brethren. It won't do us much good to talk about our "love" problem unless we are all defining love the way Jesus does. His is the love we are to model, so His is the love we must understand.

Jason R. Velotta

Chapter 2

What is Love?
(Baby don't hurt me, don't
hurt me....no more)

S omeone once said, "love is never having to say you are sorry"...what a load of bull! Try that and see how it turns out! It would be more accurate to say, "love means *always* having to say you're sorry," (even when you're not wrong.) In fact, I never really understood how sorry I was until I committed to love someone. My wife categorically rejects any definition of love that means I never have to say I'm sorry. But honestly, because I love her, I want to say I'm sorry. Love is strange that way. Love can make you happy or it can hurt you deeply. Love can cause you to give sacrificially or it can cause you to do very selfish things. If you ask 4 different people to define love, you will get 5 different answers. So we must have a biblical definition of this "love" that causes some people to hurt and others to leap with joy. We can't simply assume we are all talking about the same thing when we use the word, "love."

I used to think I understood love. I even preached a few messages about love, confidently asserting my view. "Love is much more than a feeling," is something I thundered from the pulpit many times. I have always known love is more than just a feeling. The Bible is clear on that, but I swung too far in the other direction with my view of love. For me, love was a commitment, but love was nothing more than a commitment. I would have never blatantly said love is nothing but a commitment, but that's what I thought. Since then, my perception of love has changed. I still believe love is much more than a feeling and I still believe love is a commitment, but that is not the whole story. Unfortunately, it took a dog named Max to help me learn this lesson. Max was a sixteen-week-old Puggle. I remember being embarrassed to tell people Max was a Puggle. What a goofy name for a dog breed. A Puggle is part Pug and part Beagle, hence the name. Max was irresistibly cute and my children absolutely loved him. I, on the other hand, wasn't that fond of Max. Every night Max spent all his energy trying to get out of his pen. His sole purpose in life was to escape his kennel and use the bathroom all over my house. Max was what I call a marathon pooper. He wouldn't just leave a single pile for us to clean. He would leave fourteen piles all over the house in the space of a few hours.

Needless to say, Max and I didn't get along. I love dogs but I can't stand a dog messing in my house. So in the course of a few weeks, we tried many different tactics to housebreak Max. Nothing seemed to work. As I look back on the whole situation, I can't help but think Max was mentally handicapped. Anyway, because of all the turmoil he was causing in my house, the church heard more than a few sermons using Max as an illustration. Although it sounds shamefully ridiculous now, I actually compared the love of Christ to the love I showed that dog. I had taken the dog into my house, fed it, and committed to care for it even though the dog did nothing but defile everything I had given it.[9] The point of the sermon came to a head when I showed the congregation that love is a commitment, not just a fuzzy feeling. I had committed to love Max regardless of how much he desecrated my house. My children loved him, so I committed to love him. At the time, I thought it was a pretty good illustration. Jesus has committed himself to love us and the Father loves us because of the Son. His love is unconditional and we tend to insult it with our sin and disobedience. Obviously I thought my love for the dog was also unconditional because he sure didn't deserve it.

The week after I preached the sermon using Max as an illustration we tried a new potty training tactic. We decided to lock Max up in a smaller kennel while we were gone and immediately let him outside when we returned home. This way, he would learn to do his business outside. We thought he surely wouldn't sully his tiny kennel. There simply wasn't enough room to move around in there. Little did we know that we hadn't yet reached the bounds of Max's

---

[9] "Defile" is a very polite way to describe what that dog did!

determination. Three days in a row, Max not only pooped in the kennel, but he playfully rolled around in it before we got home. For three straight days I returned home and had to take the dog out of his kennel to wash feces off him. On the third day, I found out just how conditional my love was for Max. Rolling around in dog mess was the straw that broke the camel's back.

We spent $250 on Max, not counting all the shots and pet supplies. When I took him back to the pet store, the lady behind the counter politely said, "I'm sorry we don't give refunds." I let her know very quickly that I didn't care about a refund. They just needed to take the dog back. She said, "We don't usually take pets back once they are sold," insinuating that I should try to find some other way to relieve my self of Max (who now freshly smelled like Dawn dishwashing liquid.) Her eyes widened when I told her they would either take the dog back or I would leash him to the store's outside door handle when I left. So, they graciously took the dog back...and also kept my $250. Problem solved.

A few weeks later, people from the church were still talking about my "love" sermon involving Max the friendly poop machine. Quite a few were shocked when I told them I must not have loved Max as much as I had claimed. I committed to love that dog, but my commitment could only stand so many poops. My love for him was very conditional. In that moment, I realized that love is a huge commitment, but commitment is not all love is. True love is much, much more than that.

Although love is not easy to explain, we all have some

idea about love's nature. Maybe you have never purposefully tried to define love, but on some level we all have an idea about what love is. Unfortunately, different people define love in very different ways. Some see love as an overriding emotion that must be sought after and possessed. Others find that love is an involuntary emotion, not able to be managed. In this view, love either happens or it doesn't.

On the other hand, some see love as nothing more than sacrificial action on someone's behalf. For them, the heart attitude is irrelevant. Love is identified by the actions in which it engages. In addition to all this, there are certainly different kinds of love. A man loves his wife in a different way than he loves other men's wives (or at least he should.) Likewise, a man will also love his children in a different way than he loves his wife. Jesus calls us to love all mankind, but we are not to love all men the same way we love our own children. There is also another love we have for enjoyable activities. You might hear a man telling you he loves his wife and later that same man will also say he loves fishing. Is his love for his wife the same kind of love he has for fishing? Surely the man's wife hopes it isn't. This is the problem we need to address before we can talk about loving Jesus' Bride. The issue here is that, as followers of Christ, we are commanded by our master to love His church. How are we supposed to do that when that very church can often be hurtful and vindictive? What kind of love should we be giving? A heartfelt emotion? Sacrificial action? Loving people from a distance?

The number of definitions one could ascribe to love seems almost infinite. So the only definition of love that matters in our current study is Jesus' definition. We must be resolved to understand what Jesus considers love to be. He is the one who commands us to love the brethren, so his idea of love is the one we must accept and obey. It really doesn't matter what the lady next-door thinks love is. Her definition won't be the one by which we are judged. We can easily formulate our own definition of love, but unless it accords with Scripture, our definition is useless. What Jesus thinks about love is our only concern because His commands are what we must keep.

No student of the Bible can doubt that we are called to love all men, even our enemies. But Jesus tells believers specifically, "A new commandment I give to you, that you love one another, even as I have loved you, that you also love one another" (John 13:34.) Likewise, the Apostle John tells us that love for the brethren is an evidence of salvation itself (1 John 3:14.) So as followers of Jesus, we must be very careful to define love correctly. Christ surely commands a true love, so if our definition of love is narrowed to fit our own tendencies, we might be living disobediently. If we think love is something different from what Christ thinks, we are wrong. Even more frightening, if we are confident in a false definition of love, we may be resting in an assurance of salvation that is not real. Our definition of love is supremely important. Therefore before we can address the problem of loving the brethren, we must understand what Jesus means by love.

In church life, it doesn't take long before someone hurts or offends you. That's just our nature. People in the church are sinners just like everyone else and they can be very hurtful. So when they mistreat me, I know that Jesus has called me to love them anyway. But what does that actually mean? Does it mean I am required to be nice to them? Does it mean I must allow them another opportunity to hurt me? There are so many practical questions about loving the brethren that it isn't easy to know exactly where to start. Many people define love as simply caring more for someone else than one does for himself/herself. There is some truth to this and we can all see how this characterizes love, but this definition isn't perfect. It is very possible to care deeply about someone, even more than oneself, and not actually love him or her. Love is so difficult to define that some people, like Dr. Deborah Anapol think:

"Love is a force of nature…love is bigger than you are. You can invite love, but you cannot dictate how, when, and where love expresses itself. You can choose to surrender to love, or not, but in the end love strikes like lightening, unpredictable and irrefutable."[10]

If she is correct how can love be commanded? How can Jesus demand that we love His bride when love itself is

---

[10] Deborah Anapol Ph.D. "What is Love, and What Isn't?" *Psychology Today*, Nov. 25, 2011.

https://www.psychologytoday.com/blog/love-without-limits/201111/what-is-love-and-what-isnt?collection=1070853 (Accessed 5/17/15) beyond our control? But if love is within our control, how can it be truly heartfelt? How can I make my heart love someone? Before we look at what the Bible says about love and our responsibility, it may be helpful to begin by showing what love is not.

What love is Not

Love is Not Just Passive

With all due respect to Dr. Anapol, love doesn't just fall out of the sky. Especially when it comes to romantic love, most people think, "The heart wants what the heart wants." Thinking love is a passive force that hits you when you least expect is how most people view love. Love strikes like lightening and no one can predict where and when it hits. Even if we are talking about loving the church instead of romantic love, the idea that individuals cannot help whom they love is common. Even in the church, people can be tiresome and aggravating. (Yes, I said it!)[11] Regardless of who you are, I'm sure you would agree that some people are just hard to love.

By nature, mankind is selfish and arrogant. We tend to think we are unable to love those kinds of people (though many of us *are* those kinds of people.) Even when we try, there is something inside us that rebels against the idea. Try

---

[11] A friend of mine is fond of saying, "Some people are just like a slinky. They aren't good for much but they make you smile when you push them down the stairs." I'm not sure I would go that far, but it makes me laugh.

as we might to suppress it, that animosity continues to return. Because of this tendency, many people believe like Dr. Anapol…love is a force of nature. It's something that happens unexpectedly and powerfully in our hearts. Love can't be controlled or restrained. It cannot be demanded or refined. You either love a person or you don't, and if you don't, there is nothing you can do about it.

But from a biblical perspective, how can this be? If love isn't something we can manifest, how could Jesus expect us to do it? In fact, the further you go back in the biblical record, the more you see the importance of love. Jesus summed up the entire law of the Old Testament in two simple commands, "You shall love the Lord your God with all your heart, and with all your soul, and with all your mind.' This is the great and foremost commandment. The second is like it, 'You shall love your neighbor as yourself.' On these two commandments depend the whole Law and the Prophets" (Matt. 22:37-40.) But what if your neighbor is an idiot? Is it possible to love him even when my heart rebels? What if your neighbor is always purposefully antagonizing you and driving you crazy? Did Jesus mean we are to love him too?

There is a sense in which loving people the way Jesus commands is impossible for the natural man. Before salvation, no man is able to love as Christ commands. Earlier, we referenced 1 John 3:14 which says, "We know we have passed from death to life because we love the brethren." In verse 13 of that section, John specifically tells believers not to be surprised that the world hates them. Here the lines are definitively drawn. Those who are of the world hate those who are in Christ. Simply put, before a man is born again he has a natural enmity against God's people. Of course, he may not spew hatred and outward rage against the church, but internally he despises anything that reminds him of his sin and his fallen state. This man cannot bear to place himself under the authority of the one true God. The only option for the lost man is to be regenerated and when that happens, John says the man will switch teams. No longer will he be hateful toward Christ's church but he will become part of this church that the world hates. So the unsaved man can wait indefinitely for this love to passively overcome him. However, until the Spirit indwells him through conversion, it will not happen.

In this sense, the love Christ requires is not something summoned upon command as if natural men are able to change their very hearts. The new heart desires to be with God's people. Believers desire to fellowship with each other and take part in each other's lives. So when I say love is not passive, it doesn't mean that love is something you generate solely within yourself. What I mean is that even though believers have a new loving heart, there will always be people who provoke you and rub you the wrong way. There will be people in the body who will inevitably hurt your feelings, offend you in some way, or aggravate you. For believers, loving these individuals is not a passive action by any stretch of the imagination. In fact, it can be downright exhausting.

For example, we all have that person who only comes around when he or she needs something. This person never just stops by to show their love. It's always about what you can do for them (you know who that person is.) After the first three hundred times they come to you in need, your knee-jerk reaction is, "Oh great, what do you want now." We may politely listen to what they have to say, smile a lot, and nod with that compassionate look on our faces, but inside we just want the conversation to end. What would Jesus want us to do here? Of course, he calls us to forgive people not seven times but seventy times seven (which means limitless.) For me, fighting against those internal feelings while I politely and compassionately nod is not passive. I promise you it doesn't just happen. It takes a great deal of active effort and it most certainly doesn't come easy.

So a love for the brethren comes from God's love, which is shed abroad in our hearts. But that love (if it is to be a sincere love) requires active maintenance and effort. It requires us to restrain our selfish hearts and our indifferent attitudes. We are called to wrestle our resentment to the ground and hold it in submission. Sometimes we aren't even trying to be selfish or mean. There are times when we are just weary and cannot add anything else to our plate. A person comes to us in need (for the three-hundredth time) and we just don't have any more emotion left to give. It may seem reasonable to simply "be nice" in these instances without actually loving, but the root of that action is still sin. We think we deserve some time to ourselves...we deserve to be free of another's burden. Later in this chapter we will see that one of love's attributes is to "suffer long," meaning that even when weariness is there...love is still love.

This kind of love does not fall out of the sky and it is surely not easily accomplished. There are times when the last thing we want is to hear the same old story from the same old person who has thrown us under the bus countless times. To love this person takes energy and effort...lots of energy and effort. This kind of love for the brethren doesn't just happen. It isn't passive.

Love is Not Just Emotion

In many romantic movies, the greatest prize one can attain is a perfect love which fills your heart with joy. I once spoke to a group of teenagers about the dangers of watching movies like *Twilight*. In this particular movie, the lead female character, Bella, falls in love with a young vampire boy named Edward. There are many different plots and sub-plots in the film but it all boils down to a love story. Many people asked me why I thought it wasn't good for teenagers to see movies like these. Most people thought it was because of the presence of cultic imagery and monsters, but that's not why I warned them. I told one mother, "I am not worried about your daughter becoming a vampire or falling in love with a vampire." Vampires don't exist so it is foolish to worry about that. What does bother me, however, is that young ladies will be searching their entire lives for their own pasty effeminate "vampire" boyfriend and they will measure every real man by the picture of what Hollywood says "true love" looks like. And of course, when the real man doesn't measure up to how Edward loves Bella, his love must not be real love.

These Hollywood caricatures stem from the belief that love is nothing more than a heart-felt emotion. Do you remember that exhilarating feeling when you first fell in love? Unless that feeling is present at all times, people think they aren't experiencing true love. For this reason, people who have been married for many years finally give up, saying they have "fallen out of love." But true love is not something you fall into or out of. Love is something you give and receive. So many newlyweds discover after a few years of marriage (less time in some cases) that the spectacular feeling of awe and wonder tends to diminish. The couple begins getting used to each other. When this happens, many people panic because they feel like love is evaporating from their relationship. I think the opposite is true. When that spark of excitement wanes, that's when two people truly start loving each other. You might live on desire and infatuation for a while, but these things are never permanent sources of strength. Emotional excitement is not a concrete foundation on which anything can be built. Sooner or later real love must take its place. Of course, we shouldn't think love is devoid of desire, infatuation, or any number of powerful feelings – of course love manifests these things. But love is much more than just these feelings. Depending on the circumstances of life, your feelings ebb and flow like the ocean's tide. A sincere love for someone does not take outward circumstances into account (or at least it shouldn't...we will soon realize that often our imperfect love does.)

Regardless of emotion, love always motivates action. It is

not simply how a person feels. Abusive husbands all over the world claim they love their wives. I'm sure everyone would agree that a man who beats his wife doesn't really love her. But what if he really does have those feelings of desire, infatuation, and longing for her? He just can't control his behavior. If love is nothing more than the feeling he has in his heart, then maybe he really does love her. Surely you see the flaw in that logic. True love never results in abusive action. A real "heart-felt" love will always reveal itself in loving action. This is perfectly modeled in the love God has for the world. Just about everyone knows John 3:16, "For God so love the world that He gave..." God's love always manifests in His actions. Likewise, 1 John 3:17 questions those who say they love without any active demonstration in their lives. The verse says, "But whoever has the world's goods, and sees his brother in need and closes his heart against him, how does the love of God abide in him?" John's question is simple. How can you possibly think that the love of God is living inside you when you close your heart to your brother's needs? Scripture's implication is that a true love from God always expresses itself outwardly.

Later we will look at the closest thing to a definition of love we have from the Bible. In 1 Corinthians 13, Paul describes love by telling us the actions love takes. We will see that although the English translation of these texts describes love with adjectives, the actual Greek text is a list of actions. Love does things. Love is proven by the actions it produces. It is not just the feeling you have about someone. Love is not just a state of being or an emotion. Love is action.

But...

Love is Not Just Action

At the risk of contradicting myself, let me also say that love is not action alone. A person may do many good things for people and still not love them. Unfortunately, I have personal experience in this particular area. As a hospital Chaplain, part of my job is to visit with the sick. Most of my day is spent going into hospital rooms, praying with people, and counseling people through difficult times. Besides teaching God's word and pastoring people, working at the hospital is something I really love doing.

I visit some patients that illicit compassion and empathy as I hear their stories and listen to their needs. I often find myself swept up in their cares as I call out to God on their behalf. Sometimes I feel as if it were my own family member going through their great trial. There are times when I can literally feel the mother's pain who has just lost a child. Frequently, I have to go hide in the chapel and pray for strength and wisdom. I'm simply not able to bear the weight of everyone's needs. During these times, I am more alert to the fact that God is teaching me the depths of His love.

However, sometimes I worry about my own heart as I move from room to room in the hospital. There are times when I can't stop thinking about my own concerns as I pray for hospital patients. Some days, I just can't wait to clock out and go home as I counsel people in their suffering. Is this love? At times, I have caught myself saying the exact same prayer, using the exact same words, in every hospital room I entered. Did I really speak to God for those people or were my words just formulaic prayers I am being paid to say? Sometimes I don't feel anything at all when I visit with hospital patients. Like anything else, it quickly becomes just a job and not a calling. Instead of being the comforting hands and feet of God, I'm just a normal guy waiting on the clock to run out so I can go home.

In these times, I am still doing the same activities I have always done. I am going to where sick people are and I am praying for them, trying to comfort them, and bringing them the gospel – but I know in my heart that I do not really love them like I should. Just because my actions are what someone who loves would do, it doesn't necessarily mean I am showing love. It is possible to act in a loving way without actually loving people. So we cannot say that because love results in certain actions, doing these certain actions equals love. The act of doing a service doesn't always mean that love is the motivation for the service. Some people are kind to others because they believe it is their duty to be kind. Others believe they will receive a karma-like reward if they help others. These acts are motivated by selfishness rather than love and cannot be definitional to love itself.

Even in his chapter about love, the Apostle Paul said, "And if I give all my possessions to feed the poor, and if I surrender my body to be burned, but do not have love, it profits me nothing" (1 Co. 13:3.) The actions Paul describes here are loving actions. I don't know anyone who has given everything they own to feed the poor. People today have a hard time giving anything at all (myself included.) To give everything means to put everyone else's well-being above your own life. Wow! That is an enormous sacrifice. But here Paul says it is possible to do this great deed without actually loving people. He says that even if he were to give everything he had to the poor, if it wasn't motivated from a true love, it is meaningless. For Paul, love can't simply be relegated to a generous action. There must be something more. He says he could give his life away and not have love. But didn't Jesus say, "Greater love has no one than this, that one lay down his life for his friends" (John 15:13.) Doesn't this mean that laying one's life down is the greatest love imaginable? Possibly, but Paul says that one might lay down his life and have no love at all. Love results in action. There is no doubt about that. But love cannot be just action, it must be something more. Action without love is empty according to Scripture, so love cannot be defined as outwardly doing sacrificial things.

Love is Not Just Being Nice

Although it should be obvious that love is not just being nice, this particular view needs its own section. When people in the church hurt us, there is a huge temptation to grin and bear it. We try to be as nice as we can while harboring resentment in our hearts. I am reminded of a sorted tale of a church business meeting where men almost came to blows because they couldn't agree on the annual budget. From that moment on, these men had a deep-rooted hostility between them but visitors would have never known it. For these church members, the command to love one another was

fulfilled in simply putting on their church faces and smiling
when they saw one another. Outside the congregation, their
enmity festered and grew. Accusations and gossip ran
rampant among them. But even bitter enemies can be civil
to each other, especially when they see each other in church.
Being outwardly nice to someone doesn't take near the effort
that forgiving someone does.

The Apostle John tells us that the man who internally
hates his brother is a murderer, and no murderer has eternal
life (1 John 3:15.) So it doesn't really matter how nice you are
to your brother on the outside, Jesus' idea of love involves
the heart as well.

But what if you don't really hate anyone? Does that
count? Many church members aren't embroiled in the midst
of a grudge match with another member. In fact, some of the
nicest people you will ever meet go to church on Sunday.
They do not hate anyone and they are genuinely happy to be
there. They are truly "nice" to the brethren. But that is the
extent of their involvement. We will soon see that loving
someone means investing yourself in his or her well being. It
means having a heart that desires to give yourself in service
to someone else. [12] We will see this fact from Scripture
shortly. Although many people in the church are "nice,"
biblical love does not exist where church members are not
personally invested in the fellowship. Believers are called to

---

[12] Notice that this love includes both a heartfelt concern and desire for believers, as
well as a longing to invest one's life in them. This love is not exclusively emotion or
action. It is action stemming from a heart of love.

love one another, to exhort one another, and to bear one another's burdens. These commands cannot be obeyed without investing oneself in the lives of the brethren. By investing I mean being involved in people's lives and being intimately connected with them. This doesn't necessarily mean a believer must be best friends with every person in his or her particular fellowship, but it does mean that believers are called to actually fellowship with a local assembly. Fellowship doesn't just mean getting together and making idle conversation. It doesn't just mean gathering in the same building on Sunday. Fellowship (*Koinonia*, the Greek word translated fellowship) means "sharing in common" or communion with one another.

Many people show an antagonism for the brethren by simply neglecting them. They don't necessarily hate them, but they don't love them either. Some believers see no need in stretching themselves to care for people in their particular fellowship. Instead, they may sneak into the worship service and sneak out when church is over. They happily say they are members of the church and are regular attendees, but they do not actually love the brethren. For these people, regularly being nice to church people when in their company is enough.

An analogy may help at this point. Imagine if I told you I was going away for a few months. I'm going to another country and I need you to care for my wife while I am gone. Having pledged yourself to this task, I leave with the expectation that you will make sure my wife is taken care of, she is fed, and she has everything she needs. Yet, while I am gone, you do absolutely nothing to take care of her. She goes about hungry, hurting, and needing all kinds of help. But no one helps her...no one cares for her. You agreed to tend to her needs but instead you completely neglected her when she needed you most. Do you think I would be happy with you when I returned? I can assure you I would not be.

In the same way, Jesus loves his bride. Of course she can be hard for us to love. She can be hurtful and spiteful. But Jesus loves her and He left us specific instructions about how to edify and love her. When we neglect her because she can be cantankerous, we are choosing to ignore her cries for help and Jesus' specific instructions. When Jesus returns, how in the world could He be happy with the way we have treated His bride? Instead of love, we have chosen to simply be nice to her when we see her, and make a point not to see her too often.

Niceness doesn't equal love. Outwardly nice people who harbor hatred in their hearts don't love others. We all know that. Yet in a similar manner, people who choose to neglect others don't love either. Indifference might as well be hatred because it still falls short of the love Jesus commanded. But in addition to all this, we know that niceness doesn't equal love because sometimes the most loving thing a Christian can do for another is not be nice. In Matthew 18:15-18, Jesus gives his disciples specific instructions about confronting a brother who has slipped into sin. First, we are to come and plead with the brother personally. If that fails, we are to bring another with us to reason with him. Finally, if he still doesn't repent we are to take the matter before the church.

The purpose behind these actions is love. Jesus and the disciples love their brothers too much to allow them to remain in sin, but this often looks like hateful judgment to the one in sin. In this instance, being nice is the most unloving thing the believer can do.

Parents know that loving their children means having to administer tough love. This kind of love is never nice. Niceness cannot be the same as love. Therefore, fulfilling the commandment to love the brethren is much much more than simply being nice when we see them.

Love is Not Just Toleration

Toleration is the clarion call of our age. Because this cultural mindset seeps into the church, many believers think the command to love simply means they must tolerate people. To be sure, the church is full of people who are hard to love. In fact, if you can't think of someone on your church pew that is hard to love then it's probably you! So when it's too hard to be nice to abrasive people, tolerating them is the least we can do. Toleration is enduring annoying people when we can't stand to be around them. We stomach them in the name of unity and keep our real feelings to ourselves. Mother always said, "If you can't say something nice, don't say anything at all."

We shouldn't need to go in depth as to why tolerating people is not the same as loving them. It seems pretty obvious. Tolerance is not love. It simply avoids conflict in order to keep things peaceful. But in some cases loving the brethren should bring us right into the crosshairs of conflict.

The 21st century church desperately needs to understand this. In addition to dealing with difficult believers, the church is dealing more and more with people coming into the assembly spreading false doctrine. In this case, the most loving thing a Christian can do is correct improper teaching and share truth. Correcting false doctrine always causes conflict and is the total opposite of tolerance, but it is perhaps one of the most loving things believers can do. Love is not inactive when others are swayed into false teaching, which could potentially harm their soul.

In most instances, tolerance, with its various characteristics, does not equal love. Whether we are talking about solemnly tolerating fellow believers, or tolerating the heresies attacking the church, tolerance is the enemy of love.

What Is Love?

Would it surprise you to learn that the Bible never really gives an explicit definition of love? Scripture gives us examples of love, shows us the evidence love produces, and tells us how we know love, but nowhere does the Bible tell us in so many words what love actually is. 1 Corinthians 13 is as close as Scripture comes to defining love, so this is where we must begin. The thirteenth chapter of Paul's letter to Corinth is often called the "love" chapter. This section of Scripture is usually read as the centerpiece for weddings and teachings about love.

Love is patient, love is kind and is not jealous; love

does not brag and is not arrogant, does not act unbecomingly; it does not seek its own, is not provoked, does not take into account a wrong suffered, does not rejoice in unrighteousness, but rejoices with the truth; bears all things, believes all things, hopes all things, endures all things. – 1 Corinthians 13:4-7

When we read these verses in English, Paul seems to be giving a definitional description of love. "What is love?" you ask. Love is patient, love is kind, etc… and on a certain level, you can rightly say that he is describing what love is. There is indeed a very real sense in which Paul is showing us the nature of love. However, the words used in the Greek text are not adjectives. They are action verbs.[13] Paul is telling us what love does! I'm not saying that all the English translations have mistranslated these verses. On the contrary, I would probably translate the section exactly as most formal translations do.[14] In a strict word for word translation, the above text is exactly what the words mean. For the most part, they capture Paul's intent quite well. But we must also understand that Paul is telling us what love *does* more than what love is. In this section, Paul uses love as the subject of his sentences, and demonstrates that love is accomplishing the action of the verbs he uses. So Paul is describing how we

---

[13] There are also verbal participles in the text

[14] Translations that are formally equivalent are those which attempt to translate the words as closely as possible to the original. Dynamic translations try to capture the thought and sense of the original even if it means they don't translate each word exactly.

can know love when we see it.

In John chapter three, Jesus describes the work of the Spirit to Nicodemus as being like the wind. He says you cannot see the wind but you know it by the sound it makes and the effects it has (John 3:8.) It seems as if Paul is telling the Corinthians the same thing about love. He isn't giving them a definition of love, instead, he is telling them how they can know what love is by the actions and attitudes it generates. In the context, the Corinthians' fellowship was dividing on a number of issues. They were seeking to outdo each other by possessing certain spiritual gifts, and they were dividing over which teacher they should follow. The church was even divided over the behaviors of some of its members. Paul instructs them about the most important focus of the believer's life. This focus should be love. He shows them the actions love takes so they might recognize love (or the lack of it) in themselves. 1 Corinthians is specifically written to church members. The people in that church were treating each other just like many modern church members do. So we should read this section as instructing us all how to live as Christ commanded. The church is called to love, not just with emotions, but also with our lives.

It may be helpful to give you an alternative translation of this passage to illustrate what Paul is saying. In *The New International Greek Testament Commentary*, Dr. Anthony Thiselton gives an in depth analysis and exegesis of 1 Corinthians 13:4-7 and he translates the passage as follows:

Love waits patiently...shows kindness...does not

burn with envy...does not brag, and does not cherish inflated ideas of its own importance. Love does not behave with ill-mannered impropriety. It is not preoccupied with the interests of self. Love does not become exasperated into pique (anger), [or] keep a reckoning of faults. Love takes no pleasure in wrong doing but joyfully celebrates truth. Love never tires of support, never loses faith, never exhausts hope, and never gives up.[15]

Many books and sermons deal with each phrase of 1 Corinthians 13, so I don't intend to give an exhaustive commentary on the passage. Biblical scholars, far more intelligent than I, have already done that. However, because we can't learn how to love until we understand biblical love, we must examine the Bible's presentation of what love produces.

Love is patient...

As already stated, it would be more accurate to say, "love waits patiently," or "love acts with patience." Paul isn't just describing an attribute of love. He is showing us what love produces. Love, in the biblical sense, waits patiently. How patient are you? Would the people closest to you describe you as a patient person? I shudder even asking the question, knowing that it's highly doubtful many of my friends would

---

[15] Anthony C. Thiselton. "The First Epistle to the Corinthians." *The New International Greek Testament Commentary.* (Grand Rapids, MI: Eerdmans Publishing Co. 2013) 1 Corinthians 13:4-7

call me patient. To be honest, I never recognized impatience as demonstrating a lack of love. Most of the time we think our impatience is due to outward circumstances like work, bills, or stress. We may think impatience is simply a product of our circumstances, but Scripture says impatience demonstrates a sinful lack of love. Love waits patiently. We love as Christ commands when we are patient with the brethren.

Love is Kind...

Once again I find myself hanging my head. When I think about the level of kindness I show, I want to cringe. There are certainly times when I am kind to others, but there are also times when I am quite selfish. Kindness is probably not the first word that comes to mind when someone thinks of me. Sarcastic would be a better description. Unfortunately, I have yet to find the spiritual gift of sarcasm listed in the Bible. The Scripture doesn't make provision for me when I am having a bad day or when I am simply pushed beyond the limits of my patience. There is no excuse for Christians being unkind and I can't attempt to concoct one. When I am unkind, I am sinning...it's as simple as that. Loving as Christ loves means being kind even when church people are unkind to me. It's easy to be kind to those who are kind, but love is kind to all. Even when we sternly disagree with one another, unkindness is always sin.

Love does not burn with envy

We all know envy is a sin. Envy appears in many of

Paul's sin lists. To be honest, I don't find myself envying people with nice cars or houses. I don't envy those who have lots of money. Many people do envy the rich and if this is your proclivity, you are in direct violation of biblical love. But I am not off the hook just yet. Most often, I envy people when I am going through hard times and they are not. This envy is often coupled with pride when I begin to think I deserve the blessings others enjoy. This is a very dangerous attitude. When I see other people who I judge to be not as fruitful as myself (another dangerous attitude) enjoying blessing and comfort, I envy them. In fact, it's not just that I wish I enjoyed their blessings. I feel like I am owed blessing. Bitterness and resentment quickly follow. But if I truly loved my brethren, I would rejoice when they are doing well. I rejoice when my children are doing well – because I love them. Love doesn't burn with envy.

Love doesn't brag...cherish ideas of its own importance...seek its own interests

Pride is a killer. We can find pride lurking at the root of every sin. Without exception, pride destroys lives. In my life, pride is sneaky and manifests itself when I least expect it. I often find pride skulking at my heart's door after I have done something wonderful for God. Even then, sin never lets up. As soon as I sacrifice my time, money, or energy for others in Jesus' name, I start thinking, "I am a very loving person. Jesus is surely proud of me." I don't get too far down this road before I find myself on the corner of pride and boastful street. The good thing I did led my wicked heart right back into the same sin I was trying to avoid by doing good! But love surely doesn't puff itself up. Love is humbly understanding that we are to esteem others better than ourselves (Phil. 2:3.) Love also understands that outside of God's grace, we are absolutely nothing. Love isn't puffed up...ever.

"I deserve better than they do!" None of us would ever let those dreadful words come out of our mouths. But our actions often demonstrate the reality of that sentiment. Leaving menial tasks undone because they are beneath us says, "I deserve better." Making sure we are first in line at the potluck supper says, "I deserve better." Refusing to give up our free time to aid someone else says, "I deserve better." These actions are sinful because love does not inflate its own importance. Love considers others better than itself.

Love does not behave improperly (unbecomingly)

This seems like a "no-brainer." The word translated improper or unbecoming here means to behave disgracefully, dishonorably, or indecently.[16] Love doesn't behave in this manner. When you love someone, you don't dishonor or disgrace them. Imagine someone that supposedly loves you demeaning you at every opportunity. How would you feel? What counsel would you give someone in that situation? Would you tell a person suffering

---

[16] Frederick W. Danker et al., *A Greek-English Lexicon of the New Testament and Other Early Christian Literature*, 3rd ed. (Chicago, IL: University of Chicago Press, 1979) ἀσχημονέω.

such antagonism that they shouldn't worry about it because they are loved?

Interestingly enough, this also speaks to the reality of how we claim to love Jesus. I remember walking into a music store and hearing a man talking to a group of people about the Apostle Paul's conversion on the road to Damascus. I was pleasantly surprised to hear such conversation in the music store, but the rug was quickly pulled out from under me when I heard the language the man was using. Here he was in a public store, talking about biblical realities, and using curses and foul language that would have made a trucker blush. This guy was claiming to love Jesus but with every other word, he was dishonoring Jesus.

When I walked to the counter to make my purchase, the storeowner recognized me as a preacher. The belligerent man quickly asked me a biblical question, hoping I would buttress the argument he made to his friends. Before I answered, I asked him, "Are you a follower of Jesus?" He immediately said, "Yes I am." The only thing I could say was, "If you are going to use language like that, please stop telling people you are a disciple. You are making Jesus look bad." Love doesn't act unseemly or dishonor the one who is loved.

Love is not angered easily (provoked)

O.K. Now I'm getting a little worried. Love doesn't have a quick temper either? The deeper we study the biblical actions of love, the more I see how awful I am. When you think about it, being easily angered is a form of selfishness (trust me, I know.) When I am quick-tempered, it is usually because I desire something I am denied. Anger comes when I think I deserve something that isn't given. For example, one of the things that really gets me in a grumpy mood is having to dig through the laundry basket for matching socks. Who is this person who is so interested in my socks that he feels the need to steal them? Why does he only steal one sock from each pair? I absolutely hate digging through that basket trying to find socks that match. The longer I search, the more impatient and angry I get. I also find myself quick-tempered when I lose things like my wallet or my keys (which seems to happen quite often.)

Selfishness and pride lie at the root of my anger. I don't think I should have to go through these things. Someone else should be matching my socks and making sure my keys are where they are supposed to be. My lack of love demands that other people organize these things. I shouldn't have to do it. When I start feeling persecuted by my laundry basket I tend to take it out on those around me. Love doesn't do that. In fact, anger is nothing more than pride and ego being unleashed.

Love doesn't keep a record of faults

Finally! I have a definition of love I can manage…wait… never mind. Loving someone means that when they wrong you, their wrongs are forgiven and forgotten. Of course reconciliation comes when the person who wronged you repents, but a loving believer's heart forgives regardless.

Husbands and wives experience this all the time. When someone is wronged in the relationship, it doesn't take long before past wrongs start getting brought back up as justification for present behavior.

"I know I haven't cut the yard in two weeks, but at least I didn't burn dinner like you did the other night." Although the actual facts of the situation may change in your particular circumstance, everyone has had the record of their faults revisited. Nowhere is this tendency more prevalent than in the church. It sounds foolish but there are a great many people harboring grudges against the brethren because they were not greeted with a welcoming handshake when they arrived. But laying all the silly reasons to hold a grudge aside, when there is a real issue between fellow believers, love does not keep a record of it. Love sees the best in people (O.K. now I am really depressed.)

Love does not rejoice in unrighteousness but rejoices in truth

Prayer request time is one of the biggest problems with small group ministry and Sunday school. Don't get me wrong. I am highly in favor of small groups. These ministries are needed in the body of Christ to build relationships and get people invested in each other. But sometimes "prayer requests" turn into, "Can you believe what so and so did? We need to pray for them!" Some prayer requests quickly turn into gossip sessions or, at the very least, just a way to get information into other people's hands. Something inside us delights in a good scandal. We crave sinking our teeth into juicy gossip.

We even have a tendency to find a certain satisfaction when a church member falls into sin, especially when that church member has been ugly to us in the past. Our sinful hearts say, "I knew something wasn't quite right with that person." We also enjoy correcting people who have fallen into sin. I knew a Christian who zealously geared himself up to expose another brother's sin. The whole ordeal left a bad taste in my mouth. The man actually looked forward to "setting him straight" rather than approaching him humbly with a broken heart. Love doesn't get excited when a brother slips into sin. Love doesn't relish the opportunity to correct a brother. Love rejoices in truth and does not condone sin. But love never rejoices when others fall. Love rejoices when our brothers and sisters return to the truth and live by it.

Love never tires of support, never loses faith, never exhausts hope, and never gives up

Every church has those folks who always seem to be in need. (Don't act like you don't know who I am talking about.) I'm not necessarily talking about those needing money. It seems like some people come to church to specifically drain believers of their joy. For many people, being in a continuous state of sadness and trial is simply a way to get attention, a way to feel loved. They refuse to be happy and they refuse to accept wise counsel from those who lovingly give it. Fixing the problem causing their depression means losing the attention they so desperately crave. Let's face it. Some people would just rather be miserable.

It feels good to help people who are hurting. That is what we are supposed to do as believers. But what about when the same hurting people seek you out at every service? It feels like you have a target on your back. They always want to dump all their sad stories and problems on you. Honestly, it gets old pretty quick. "Can't I enjoy one service without you shoveling all your problems on me?"

But love never grows tired of supporting others. Christ supports us every moment as we continually fail him. To love like Christ is to "bear all things." This kind of love bears the burdens of our brothers and sisters even when it infringes on our own enjoyment. This kind of love believes all things. It gives people the benefit of the doubt, even if it is the thirtieth time they cry on your shoulder. Maybe they are really hurting and going through something they simply can't get away from.

Christ's love hopes in all things. It never loses hope in others. As believers in the twenty first century, we are constantly disappointed in humanity. We definitely aren't as gullible as we used to be. When people are continually in need and they reject wise council, we tend to lose hope they are worth helping. We lose hope that we can be any benefit to them. We often assume they just won't do what needs to be done in order to come out of their perpetual gloominess. This isn't love. When we lose hope in people, we sinfully refuse to love as Christ loves them.

Finally, love endures all things. No matter what our brothers and sisters do to us, we endure it as a good soldier. Any time spent in the ministry demonstrates that people will love you with all their heart when you are doing things for them. But these same people will turn on you in an instant when they don't need you anymore. Believers who love the way Christ loves endure these things with patience knowing that Christ endured the same thing.

What's the Verdict?

So now we know what love does and what it doesn't do. These are not the only explanations of love in the Scriptures but they do seem to be the most comprehensive. Philip Ryken, in his book *Loving the Way Jesus Loves* tells his readers to examine their love by 1 Corinthians 13. He tells us to put our names in the text everywhere the word love (or charity) appears. Are they true statements? Is Jason patient? Is Jason kind? Does Jason brag? Is Jason arrogant? If you put your name in those descriptions of love's actions, do they accurately describe you? If so, you are demonstrating the love of Christ in your life. You are doing exactly what Christ would have you do. If you are not living out these things, you are sinning. It's as simple as that. Failing to love is a grievous sin. Jesus said the greatest commandments were to love the Lord your God and to love your neighbor as yourself. These actions are what true love produces. They are the evidence of love. So how are you doing?

If you are honest, you will admit that you're not doing well...neither am I. In fact, we can't love in this manner without the power of the Holy Spirit and the risen Christ.

When you inserted your name into 1 Corinthians 13, you saw that none of those attributes describes your heart. Don't' feel too bad. I saw the same thing. Fortunately for us there is a name that does exemplify these characteristics perfectly. Jesus is patient. Jesus is kind. Jesus is not jealous, does not brag, and is not arrogant.

Our inability to love is why we need the gospel. Outside of Christ's love, we cannot truly love people. But even with a regenerated heart, loving people like Jesus is hard work. Forcefully making up your mind to love people is easy. "From now on I am going to love my enemies no matter what!" is a statement many people have made. Maybe you have made a commitment to God like that. But when we try to love from the sheer force of our will, we will never be able to keep our promise. Only Jesus loves like that. He alone fulfills the perfect righteousness of love and lives through us so that we may demonstrate these qualities.

So what are we supposed to think? It seems hopeless. We can't love in our own strength and we are supposed to fight to love others. How do we do that? Although it is true, it's not enough just to say Jesus does it through us. That makes it sound like loving people is completely passive and Jesus takes over our mind and body to accomplish it. That's not the way it works. So what is the answer?

Before we start making practical applications dealing with loving those people who have hurt us, we must get a solid foundation under us. Here it is. Are you ready? You are not a good person. Your heart is not good and you can do absolutely nothing to fix yourself. Biblical love is a truly frightening thing, because it's beyond our capability. This presents a colossal problem. We began our study of 1 Corinthians 13 at verse 4 because Paul begins describing love's actions there. But in verses 1-3, Paul makes it clear that love is mandatory to be fruitful for Christ in our lives. Serving Christ without loving others is no service at all!

"If I speak with the tongues of men and of angels, but do not have love, I have become a noisy gong or a clanging cymbal. If I have the gift of prophecy, and know all mysteries and all knowledge; and if I have all faith, so as to remove mountains, but do not have love, I am nothing. And if I give all my possessions to feed the poor, and if I surrender my body to be burned, but do not have love, it profits me nothing" - 1 Corinthians 13:1-3.

Paul says all his knowledge, wisdom, gifts, talents, and self-sacrifices are absolutely worthless without love. There simply is no substitute for love. Without biblical love, everything we do is useless in the kingdom of God. Pay close attention to what Paul says in verses 1 and 2. He emphatically states that even if he exhibits extraordinary gifts, if he does not have love, he is nothing. Did you get that? He said, "If I don't have love, *I am nothing*." There is no room for pride or entitlement if you find yourself lacking in love. In other words, we are all in trouble.

Why are we unable to conform to God's standard? What must we do? How can we love like Christ when the very people we are called to love hurt us so badly? Before we answer these questions we must understand the root of our problem. We must recognize why we are unable to love like Christ. Until we address the real problem, we can only treat the symptoms. We may act like we love, but what's inside us will always come out. The stresses and trials of life will make sure of that. The real problem is our hearts!

Chapter 3

What's the Problem?
Just Do it!

F rom the last chapter, I really hope you got discouraged. I bet you have never read that in a "Christian" book before. Good inspirational authors would never want you to be discouraged. But believers need to see the depths of sin before we can behold the glory of what Jesus has done in our hearts. We must address the real problem if we want to really love like Jesus. Loving people is harder than we can possibly imagine. If you read the last chapter and found that you are perfectly keeping love's requirements (especially to those who hurt you), there isn't much I can offer you. You are either completely delusional, utterly deceiving yourself, or you are Jesus. If any of these three options apply to you, there is nothing I can teach you. Side note: If you are Jesus, I just want to say, "Thanks for all you have done for me, I'm looking forward to seeing you face to face."

For those of us who have read the Bible's description of love and found ourselves desperately lacking, I want to say, "welcome to the human race." I'm so glad you could join us. No one is keeping the mandates of biblical love as Jesus commands. But wait! Does it ease your conscience to think that everyone is failing? If you feel better because no one perfectly keeps His command to love, you have missed the point of the Bible's message. Mankind is not judged based on how well others are doing. God judges men by His perfect standard. We can't just be satisfied with doing better than most people. Anything less than perfection is sin!

Understanding this, we must be careful not to fall into one of two ditches. Because the standard of love is so incredibly high, we may be tempted to think that God is satisfied if we do the best we can. This is the first ditch. Nowhere are we told, "Love one another as best as you can." Again and again, Scripture commands that we love one another as Jesus has loved us. We can't get around the obvious command to exhibit a lifestyle of sacrificial love. Lowering the Bible's standard of love is not an option.

The other ditch is the idea that we can pull ourselves up by our bootstraps and "just do it," as the Nike commercials say. You and I don't have the strength to "just do it." Have you ever set your mind to forgive someone only to find that your determination is not strong enough to accomplish the task? Nothing is more discouraging than that. As believers, we have an internal desire to keep Christ's commands and

71

love our brethren. But because of our sin, it doesn't take long before we're right back in the same position, making the same promise to God again. In my life, this recurring cycle has lead to great despair and hopelessness as I began to realize my weakness. Our will is simply not strong enough to follow Jesus…not without the Holy Spirit.

Why is "love" so hard?

In the last chapter I dropped a bombshell on you. In case you missed it, I said, "You are not a good person." Everything inside us wants to think we are good, but it's just not true. You may indeed be "good" compared to other people, but compared to God's law, you aren't even close…and neither am I.

It's always easier to see the bad in other people. Coming to grips with our own evil hearts is much more difficult. Even the meanest people think they are good compared to everyone else. The most mean spirited man I ever met thought he was a good person. This guy's temper would blow up at the drop of a hat. But even this man, who clearly had all sorts of issues, told me he was a good person at heart. He excused his behavior and his lack of love by simply saying, "God knows my heart." We look at people like that and say, "Who does he think he is kidding?" But other people are looking at us and saying the same thing. All of us think our hearts are basically good even though our thoughts and behavior deny it. The fact that God knows our hearts should scare us to death. That's the problem. God knows our hearts are sinful and desperately wicked (Jer. 16:9.) And this doesn't just apply to those "mean" church members. This applies to all of us. The church is filled with totally depraved sinners. The only difference between a Christian and a lost man is God's grace and the indwelling Holy Spirit.

The first thing we must face is our own heart. The problem doesn't lie with the people who have hurt us, talked about us, and maligned us. The problem is not the fact that the church is full of hypocrites and ungodly people. We are the problem. You and I are the problem. Jesus had no trouble loving those who hurt Him and persecuted Him. He had no trouble loving those who accused Him of being demon possessed and maligning His ministry. There will always be sinful people, especially in the religious crowd. Jesus handled all that very well. Why can't we? The problem isn't with other sinners, even if they are wrong. The problem is our inability to give them the same grace we have received.

Face it...People Suck (present company included)

I almost titled this book, *People Suck*. Fortunately, cooler heads prevailed and wise counselors talked me out of it. I don't mean to offend with such apolitically correct language, but the shock value is necessary. Those of you who have been hurt by church people won't have a problem wholeheartedly agreeing with that fact. Yet we hesitate to include ourselves in that category. Providentially, the Bible has much to say on this subject. So if we want to understand why loving people is such a fight, we must come to grips with who we are in God's sight. You may already agree that we are sinners, but too many Christians don't understand just how deeply sin has corrupted us. Too many of us sweep our own sin under the rug while we adamantly leave churches because of other people's sin. Before we learn how to love those who are difficult to love, we must learn to see ourselves in truth. Take off the sugar coating and honestly look in the mirror.

What's wrong with these people?
(spoken in my best Seinfeld voice)

Pastors are particularly susceptible to becoming cynical and hard hearted when ministering to people. The pastor's work shouldn't really differ that much from the work of every Christian, but pastors tend to get the lion's share of needy people seeking their assistance. Don't get me wrong...this is a good thing. God molds a pastor's heart to shepherd His people through the turmoil and trials of life. They do it because they love Christ and they genuinely love people. Most of the time, pastors long to help their congregation, and the vast majority go above and beyond the call of duty to do so. But there is real danger for servants of Christ[17] to grow pessimistic and misanthropic.

Loving sinners will always be a messy business. It's

---

[17] This doesn't just apply to professional ministers. All Christians are called to disciple others and serve one another.

especially hard when some people masquerade as growing believers. Many people only come to the church when something bad happens. When their suffering ends, they go back to business as usual. They come to the church because they wanted something. When the doctor gives them bad news, they are first in line at church. Every time the doors are open, they'll be there. However, when there is no pressing need or concern hanging over their head, Christ and the church take a back seat to more pressing matters...like mowing the yard or getting some rest. When a disciple pours out his life for someone like that, it can be depressing. After you see this game played over and over again, you naturally become skeptical and reserved.

Youth ministers have also seen this happen with parents and their children. When the kids begin their teenage years, parents want them involved with the ministry of the church. They want other people's teens to model godly character and invest in their child's life. They want the youth pastor and the adult leaders to instruct their child in the Scriptures and give them a foundation for their adult life. But when those same kids turn sixteen or seventeen, their parents don't think it's important anymore. It isn't important for their kids to model godliness for the next generation. Parents no longer have need of the youth group so they don't emphasize participation and involvement anymore. These parents got what they wanted from the church and they don't need her anymore. Once their need was met, they disengaged.

Lest you think I am on my high horse denigrating church

members, I'll admit that I see that same tendency in myself. For a long time I shook my head in disgust asking, "what is wrong with these people?" I could see every splinter in peoples' eye but I never noticed the log in my own. Of course as a pastor, my selfishness didn't manifest the same way, but it was still there. I was in church whenever the congregation met. My children were there as well. As my children got older, I stressed the importance of being that light for the next group of kids. When something tragic or unforeseen happened in my life, I was already present, working and serving in the church. I was not like those other people (so I thought) and their careless unappreciative attitude toward the church rubbed me the wrong way.

But the exact same tendency I despised in those other people was taking place in my own heart. When I needed God to act in some situation, I would pray without ceasing. I spent days at a time calling out to God and searching the Scriptures. I was closer to God than I ever thought possible when I was going through some of the hardest times of my life. Then, when life presented no great trials or difficulties, I would slip back into doing the bare necessities. I still read the Scripture and prayed, but no longer did I pour out my heart in eager expectation that God would come to answer my prayers. No longer did I read the Bible intently longing for God to draw me closer to Him. Instead, my study was focused on preparing sermons for other people. In the final analysis, I am no different than everyone else. I am a selfish sinner in total need of God's unconditional grace and I habitually took that grace for granted.

I hope you are honest enough to see this in your own heart. For a long time I wasn't that honest. But why are we like this? Why do we take God for granted when we think we don't need Him? Saying we don't need God in the good times is something we would never admit, but our actions are undeniable. The reason for this is simple...we are sinners. That's easy enough to say but to delve into the depths of what that truly means is difficult. It's painful to look at ourselves through the lens of a perfectly holy God. Sin is the reason church people can be so hurtful. Sin is also the reason we feel like we must retaliate when we are wronged. Sin is why people cannot forgive those who have hurt them, and it is also why people have become experts in hurting others. Before we can inquire about loving Jesus' bride when she is hurtful, we have to understand why she is hurtful and why we think we deserve to be treated better.

Mr. Big Stuff, who do you think you are?

Let's get real. Sometimes people in the church can be just as hateful and hurtful as people in the world. Anyone serving in a local fellowship is well aware of this fact. But why is this so surprising? More than that, why does it hurt so badly when church people do it? I think the problem lies in our view of man. The doctrine of sin and our view of humanity are directly related to how we view the gospel of Christ. Later, we will see how our perception of the gospel informs everything else in our lives, but now we must focus on our view of sin and its effects.

Most people have an unbiblical view of humanity. The

"goodness" of mankind is a popular theme in our culture. If you took a survey of every person living within a fifty-mile radius of your home, you would find that the vast majority of them (even church members) believe that all people are basically good at heart. We look pretty good, especially when we compare ourselves to "really evil" people. For example, if I were to compare my life to people like Charles Manson or Adolf Hitler, I always come out smelling like a rose. Compared to those guys, I am a really good person.

You may be a really good person compared to all your friends. Realizing how good we are measured against other people makes us all feel better. Sure, I might not pray as much as I should, and I don't fanatically follow Jesus like other people, but at least I haven't murdered anyone. Of course, I've held a grudge for five years but I am a lot nicer than you. At least I haven't cheated on my spouse like my next-door neighbor! Compared to most people, I am a great person.

We have already seen that God doesn't compare us with other people. We are commanded to compare ourselves with Jesus not other sinners. How "good" are you when you compare yourself to Jesus? Measured by His standard, you aren't doing well! In fact, the Bible says there is no one who is good, not even one! (Rom. 3:10) We are not good people who occasionally make mistakes. Rather, we are criminally sinful and never do anything righteous in God's sight. Apart from the sacrifice of Christ and the indwelling of the Holy Spirit, we are totally corrupt. Oh, we may do good things by the world's standards. We may feed the homeless and help our neighbor cut the grass. We may give money without expecting anything in return. Lots of things we do can be called good. But no work is righteous before God outside of Christ. Paul said, "For I know that nothing good dwells in me, that is, in my flesh; for the willing is present in me, but the doing of the good is not" (Rom. 7:18.) No work can earn us points before a Holy God. God's righteousness demands absolute perfection. If a work isn't perfect, it isn't acceptable. Perfection doesn't accept any deed that is tainted by sin. Therefore, in our flesh we have nothing good to offer. So our "goodness" can never earn any merit before God. That is why we need a savior. Think about that for a moment. In your own power, you have never done anything pleasing to God…not even once!

Illustrating this fact from Scripture is easy. The Bible says mankind is "dead in sin" (Eph. 2:1), "slaves to sin" (John 8:34), "sold under sin" (Rom. 7:14), and in "captivity to the law of sin" (Rom. 7:23.) Of course, one of the most definitive passages regarding man's sinful heart is Romans 3:10-18:

As it is written, There is none righteous, not even one; There is none who understands, There is none who seeks for God; All have turned aside, together they have become useless; There is none who does good, There is not even one. Their throat is an open grave, With their tongues they keep deceiving, The poison of asps is under their lips; Whose mouth is full of cursing and bitterness; Their feet are swift to shed blood, Destruction and misery are in their paths, And the path of peace they have not known. There is no fear of God before their eyes.

I must confess that every time I read this section of Scripture, which is a conglomeration of quotes from the Old Testament, something rises up in me. My heart screams, "those verses aren't talking about me!" But they most certainly are. There is no one who does good...and just in case I want to side step that, Paul says, "not even one!" It's almost like he is saying, "I am talking about you, Jason." No one on the planet does anything good outside of Jesus Christ.

Passages like Genesis 6:5 show us the depths to which man sank after the world was corrupted by sin. The verse says, "Then the Lord saw that the wickedness of man was great on the earth, and that every intent of the thoughts of his heart was only evil continually." Did you hear that? Everything in man was only evil...all the time. We also find the very familiar statement of Jeremiah who says, "The heart is more deceitful than all else and is desperately sick; Who can understand it" (Jer. 17:9).

"Wait just a minute," you may say. "What about saved people...church people? Haven't their hearts been changed?" This question gets us to the root of the problem. When people darken the doors of a church for the first time, they assume they are walking into a gathering of "good" people. The world thinks church people are supposed to be righteous and oozing the love of Jesus from every pore. No wonder most people come away disappointed.

Likewise, many church members look at their congregation this way too. This is why so many fellow believers never share their sin problems with each other. In their minds, church folks aren't supposed to have sin problems! The struggle with sin is supposed to be gone. So when Christians deal with sin in their lives, they try to do it alone. In a congregation of "good" people, it's shameful to admit we still struggle. Bringing these problems out in the open would be a disgrace. Everyone would question your commitment to Jesus if you did that...and so the charade goes on.

But what does all this have to do with loving our brethren who have hurt us? I'm getting to that. The church is not filled with righteous people regardless of what some think. The body of Christ is made up of wretched sinners just like the rest of the world. There are groups of people who believe they have not sinned since their salvation, but the Bible simply doesn't support this belief. The sinner out in world living independently from God, has the same flesh as the saint who has been saved by God's grace. The difference is that the believer's heart has been changed and they hate their sin. A war against sin rages in the heart of Christ's people. Therefore, we can't just say, "We are evil sinners" and leave it at that. If we are truly born again, the Spirit within us wrestles against our sin and hates its very presence. Our hearts are desperately wicked, but the Holy Spirit in us produces a supernatural love for God that despises the flesh (Gal. 5:17.)

God's grace is the only difference between true Christians and the lost world. While all men (lost or saved) still reside in their fleshly bodies, believers have received a new nature. Those in Christ have the Holy Spirit inside them and have become a new creation. No longer are we slaves to the sin that corrupted humanity from the time of Adam's fall. Christians have been freed from that slavery and serve Christ as their new master. Yet the flesh has not disappeared. Even believers still have sinful, selfish desires...and yes believers still commit sinful acts. God's people are perfected in God's sight from the moment Christ saves them, but the process of practically becoming like Christ takes a lifetime. It takes growth. This process of being conformed to the image of God's Son is called sanctification. Sanctification won't be completed until believers are glorified in the presence of Christ himself (Phil. 1:6.)

So we finally come to the point. If I am a member of a church fellowship, I should readily understand that the brethren with whom I serve are wretched sinners just like me. They have selfish hearts just like me, and they want what's best for them...just like me. The only thing that unites us is the union we share with Christ. Inside every believer there is a war raging. This war never takes a break and there are no cease-fires. The Spirit inside us battles the sinful flesh and this struggle is relentlessly continual. Lest we think this is some abnormal experience for weak believers, we should hear Paul's words in Romans chapter 7. Let Paul explain the struggle going on inside him as an Apostle of the Lord Jesus Christ. He desires to do good because of his new nature, but evil is still present with him causing him to do the things he knows are wrong. Please read these verses carefully. Read them as if you have never seen them before. Understanding the struggle going on inside Paul will shed light on the struggle all believers face. Romans 7:14-23 reads:

> For we know that the Law is spiritual, but I am of flesh, sold into bondage to sin. For what I am doing, I do not understand; for I am not practicing what I would like to do, but I am doing the very thing I hate. But if I do the very thing I do not want to do, I agree with the Law, confessing that the Law is good. So now, no longer am I the one doing it, but sin which dwells in me. For I know that nothing good dwells in me, that is, in my flesh; for the willing is present in me, but the doing of the good is not. For the good that I want, I do not do, but I practice the very evil that I do not want. But if I am doing the very thing I do not want, I am no longer the one doing it, but sin which dwells in me.
>
> I find then the principle that evil is present in me, the one who wants to do good. For I joyfully concur with the law of God in the inner man, but I see a different law in the members of my body, waging war against the law of my mind and making me a prisoner of the law of sin which is in my members.

This war between flesh and Spirit is important for us to understand. Every saved person is fighting this battle. If you are a follower of Christ, you see that struggle inside you. But that same struggle is taking place in our brothers and sisters as well. Sin is why sincere church people can be hurtful and also why you and I are so adamant about the fact that we deserve to be treated rightly. All of us have an innate selfishness that is continually being purged from our heart. Some of us are farther along than others and it shows in the way we behave. But we are all on the road of sanctification somewhere. None of us have arrived yet.

You would never criticize a blind man for stepping on your toes, would you? Of course not, he is blind. Likewise, you probably wouldn't harbor hard feelings against a deaf man because he ignored you when you spoke. But we expect God's people, who are continually fighting against the flesh to always treat us perfectly. We all have a tendency to desire mercy for ourselves yet demand justice for others. It shouldn't be surprising that sinners eventually sin against us. There are times when the flesh gets the better of us and we find ourselves acting in ways that Christ would never act. Why don't we sympathize with people when they do the same? We don't sympathize because we are sinners too. We deserve better, don't we? We deserve to be treated rightly and we will take nothing short of perfection when it comes to how others interact with us. It's a vicious cycle. Other people's sin offends us. We are offended because our sin says we deserve better. Then we retaliate by sinning against others. We can't break this pattern until we realize that we are all in the same boat. All of us are wicked sinners, being daily sanctified by God's Spirit.

The Body Shop

An illustration may help to get this point across. I used to paint cars in a body shop. The first man I worked for specialized in restoring old cars to their original state.

Sometimes the cars were fancy classics and sometimes they were just wrecks needing to be rebuilt. If there is one thing I grew to hate it was restoring those old classics. Fixing a damaged car is different – you pull out a few dents, replace a few parts, and paint the car. The car comes in the front door and in a few days it's headed back out. Restorations are not like that. They usually take many months if not years. The car has to be stripped down to its bare metal skeleton and rebuilt from the ground up. You never really know what you are getting into when you take on a project like that. A car that looks decent on the outside may be riddled with hidden rust underneath. The best you can do is hope there isn't too much unseen damage when you begin working.

That's how we are when we come to Christ. Jesus doesn't just fix a few dents, throw on a new paint job and send us back out the door. He completely rebuilds us from the ground up. He remakes us into new creatures and begins building us upon this new foundation.

I remember working on an old Chevy Chevelle when I was learning to do body work. The term *rust bucket* doesn't even begin to describe this car. Most people would have parked it in a field and let the grass grow around it. It was that bad! But we were just students and the vocational school offered incredibly low prices so people would donate cars for us to practice on. The man who owned the Chevelle was getting a great deal. The very first thing we did was strip the car down to the bare skeleton. We took off the doors, the fenders, the quarter panels, and even cut out part of the trunk. This guy's car went from a rolling rust bucket to a pile of rusty metal. Needless to say, the owner of the car was pretty distressed when he saw it. He didn't really understand how a group of kids could build a show car from this heap of metal. In his mind, we had destroyed his car.

What I remember most about that experience was the habitual visits the owner made to the shop. He stopped by every other day hoping to see some progress being made on his car. Day after day he left disappointed. He couldn't see a glimmer of what the finished product would look like. After awhile, he decided we were moving too slowly for him and he got very angry. We were working on his car faithfully but it wasn't a show car by any stretch of the imagination. The Chevelle was slowly being transformed from a hunk of useless metal into a drivable automobile. But every day the owner came to the shop expecting to see his "show car," and every day what he saw disappointed him. The work was being done, but it was nowhere near finished yet.

This is how we look at church folks. We expect Christian people to be a righteous "show car" for Jesus when in reality, Jesus is still working on them. He is daily sanctifying us and changing us into His image. But the work is nowhere near finished. When that rusty spot shows up in someone's attitude, instead of understanding that Jesus is still working on them, we denigrate them for not being a "show car." We expect people to be perfect in word, thought, and deed toward us. Consequently, just like the owner of that old Chevelle, we are disappointed time and time again when all we can see is a work in progress.

But there is still more to the story. Even if people treat us like dirt, shouldn't we still be able to love them like Jesus? Isn't that the call of the Christian? Why do we get so disappointed and angry when people are offensive to us? Shouldn't we model Jesus' actions by forgiving and loving them? Absolutely we should! Then why don't we? The answer to this question is the same as before. We don't love and forgive because we are also sinners at heart. Our fleshly hearts tell us we deserve to be treated perfectly. Our sinful desires demand that we be treated with the utmost respect and it is shameful when someone fails to do so. The same thing we despise in others (sin) is the thing causing us to be bitter and resentful! But, Jesus is still working on us too! We are still sinful and there is a war going on in us. The flesh and the Spirit are doing battle inside our hearts as well as every believer. When we are persecuted, maligned, or mistreated, the flesh rises up and says, "How dare they treat me like that! Those people are supposed to be Christians. What kind of church is this anyway?" Sin causes others to hurt us and our sin causes us to think we deserve better.

Yet, Paul (the same Paul who struggled so much with sin in Romans 7) told us that as believers, we are to "Do nothing from selfishness or empty conceit, but with humility of mind regard one another as more important than yourselves; do not merely look out for your own personal interests, but also for the interests of others" (Phil. 2:4-5.) Notice what he says here. He doesn't just give us the golden rule, "Do unto others as you want them to do unto you." Here he gives us what I call the platinum rule, "regard one another as more important than yourselves..." What if we really did that? When others hurt us, would we be offended if we thought of them as more important than ourselves?

The reason it's hard to love others is because we are just as sinful as they are. All Christians are fighting that same battle with sin. The Holy Spirit inside us is guiding us toward good deeds and leading us to love each other unselfishly. Yet at the same time, our flesh is still present with us and it loves to fan the flames of our selfish desires. We should not be surprised that church people can sometimes be extremely hurtful and we should also not be surprised that we are so easily offended. The reason for both problems is the same...sin.

Our flesh lives by the same rules that toddlers in the nursery live by:

If I like it...it's mine

If it's in my hand...it's mine

If I can take it from you...it's mine

If I had it a little while ago...it's mine

If it's mine...it must never appear to be yours in any way

If I'm doing or building something...all the pieces are mine

If it looks just like mine...it's mine

If I saw it first...it's mine

If you're playing with it and you put it down...it's mine

If it's broken...it's yours.

Of course in the church context, we aren't talking about toys. We are talking about selfish motives and attitudes. We are talking about respect and esteem. Our sinful desires manifest themselves in the way we serve, the way we interact, and the way we try to always come out on top. It all boils down to the same thing...sin. Sin is the reason others will never treat us with perfect goodness. Sin is also the reason we feel we deserve to be treated with perfect goodness. In the same way, it is our sin that keeps us from accepting that believers are not yet perfect and all of us have the tendency to hurt one another.

When we come to understand that sin is the root of the entire problem, we will start to see the only viable solution. When we are mistreated or maligned, our solution is to either to lash out or simply disconnect. We either desire justice for the wrong done to us or we administer the "silent treatment" to prove our point. But rather than being a resolution to our hurt, these things simply add to the pressure boiling inside us. Instead of a solution, retaliation of any kind adds to the problem.

Since sin is the root cause on both sides of the conflict, the only possible solution for dealing with "church hurt" is the gospel. You and I cannot change other people. No amount of vindictive action, silent treatment, or neglected fellowship can ease the pain in your heart...only the gospel of Jesus can do that. All we can do is address the sin in our own hearts. It's that sin causing us to hold onto resentment and bitterness. Dwelling on how the other party is not living up to their Christian duty is a fruitless enterprise. The only productive option is to work on ourselves. The only healing option is to apply the gospel to our own sinful hearts

Jason R. Velotta

regardless of what any other church member does.

Chapter 4

The Gospel Centered Love

This is usually where people run into problems. We have heard Jesus' non-negotiable command to love the brethren. Scripture has also taught us that this love is not just an outward action, nor is it just an emotion. Biblical love always takes action, but it always does so with a heart of compassion and service.

Right about now you should be feeling a little disheartened. I hope you are already protesting about the impossibility of this kind of love. If you see the demand Christ places on His disciples and find your heart incapable of fulfilling that demand…you are exactly where you should be! Jesus brings His audience to this same point in the Sermon on the Mount. Despite much popular opinion, Jesus did not come to do away with God's law. He came to raise the bar of God's law to a higher standard. The people listening to Jesus needed to see that God's law is impossible for sinners. Only then would they recognize their need for a savior.

For example, the Jewish people had long heard the command, "You shall not commit adultery." This was one of the Commandments on which the Jewish faith was built. God Himself gave this command from Mount Sinai. Yet, many first century Jewish leaders thought abstaining from the outward act of adultery was fulfilling that law. In the Sermon on the Mount, Jesus said, "You have heard that it was said, 'You shall not commit adultery'; but I say to you that everyone who looks at a woman with lust for her has already committed adultery with her in his heart" (Matt. 5:27-28.) Jesus made the law harder! He explained the original intent of God's commands. These are heart commands. Instead of simply obeying the letter of the law by not committing adultery, Jesus said a person could break this directive with his thoughts! In the same sermon, Jesus also said whoever is angry with his brother is guilty of murder. Needless to say, I'm sure the people listening to Jesus weren't exactly filled with hope. Jesus was demonstrating the depths of their sin!

That is the point. God's law is intended to convict us. We will always look into the mirror of the law and see the ugly sin in our hearts. The law shows us our guilt so we will rush headlong to the savior, who has paid our penalty with His atoning death. The Apostle Paul said it this way. "Therefore the Law has become our tutor to lead us to Christ, so that we may be justified by faith. But now that faith has come, we are no longer under a tutor" (Gal. 3:24-25.) The law shows us who we really are. It pushes us toward the only hope we have for right relationship with the Father. When Paul says we are no longer under the tutor of the law, he doesn't mean it is now acceptable to murder and commit adultery. He means that now we are free from the condemnation of the law. Believers are free to obey God's commands out of love rather than fear.

When we hear God's expectations of our love, a feeling of dread should awaken in us. That conviction comes because we know, in and of ourselves, we are totally unable to love as God demands. But that same hopeless longing should drive us to depend on the one who *is* able to love like that. We don't despair about our inability, we trust in the one who is able. If we strive to keep the commandments in order to earn brownie points with God, we will quickly be overcome by the impossibility. Loving God with all your heart and loving your neighbor as yourself may sound simple, but putting it into practice is extremely difficult. And to obey perfectly is hopeless. Measured against our ability, the standard of perfection is so outrageous there is no hope for us to keep it. Jesus is the only one who has ever loved God and neighbor like that! Therefore, it is Christ who must love through us. In our own flesh we are powerless to keep the command to love.

Baby Steps?

I have been very vocal about the failure of the modern Christian mindset (I use the term "Christian" loosely.) Today, many think exploring the gospel of Christ is just the baby steps of the Christian life. The perfection of what Christ did for His people is not just the doorway into the Christian faith…it *is* the Christian faith. The good news is not just the first step toward living in right relationship with God. The gospel is our relationship with God. Today, we are told we need a deeper spirituality to grow closer to the Father. Bombarded with spiritual principles and self-help methods, we are always striving for what Christ has already provided. The gospel is not Christianity 101, offering nothing to the serious minded disciple. On the contrary, our salvation is the deepest level of relationship we can enjoy. The gospel is our perfection before the Father.

"Christian living," books fly off the shelves of bookstores. Applying life-coaching principles is the new norm for discipleship. Many teach that the gospel is just "milk" to be fed to new believers. Today, people want the "meat" we often hear about. Meat, we think, is the deeper things of God. We want to know the spiritual steps that bring us closer to God. We agree that what Christ actually accomplished on the cross is important, but most of us just don't understand how the truth of Jesus' sacrifice applies to our daily walk. So, deep reflection on salvation itself is considered an academic exercise. Biblical scholars study the finer points of theology, but it really doesn't affect my daily life. What a tragedy for us! Unless we understand the depths of the gospel's practical significance in our lives, we will never live in the power of the Holy Spirit, and we will never even begin to love like Jesus. The gospel is not just a set of facts to be learned. Salvation is not just the entrance of Christian faith.

The good news is the very center of our lives and it is the one truth that continually transforms us as we deepen our understanding of it.

Before we examine the gospel's all-important role in transforming our hearts to love one another, we must substantially define the gospel and then demonstrate its power to give us forgiving hearts. Please don't fall into the trap of thinking you already know everything about the gospel. A lifetime of contemplative study is insufficient to exhaust the riches of the simple message of Jesus Christ. If we don't understand and walk in this truth, love will always be joyless and laborious.

Defining the Gospel

Despite what you may have heard, the gospel doesn't start with the death of Jesus. It starts all the way back in the Garden of Eden. When Adam disobeyed God by eating from the forbidden tree, he acted as mankind's representative before the Lord. From his single act of disobedience, all of creation was plunged into the curse of wickedness and death. Because God is holy, sin separated man from his creator. This state has continued to our own time. As human beings, you and I inherit the curse of sin. Romans 5:12 says, "Therefore, just as through one man sin entered into the world, and death through sin, and so death spread to all men, because all sinned." (See also 1 Co. 15:22)

Earlier in this book we saw the Bible's description of our wickedness and, believe it or not, that is part of the gospel.

Our utter sinfulness must be a necessary part of our thinking if we are to walk in the light of the gospel. We are not good. We are not even a little bit good. Everything in us is evil, and wickedness rather than goodness defines our character. Make sure you don't miss this. It is an integral part of rightly understanding the gospel. No matter how far down the goodness scale you see yourself, you are considerably more evil than you think you are. Only against this backdrop can we see how wonderful Christ's salvation truly is. Amazingly, when we were enemies of God (Rom. 5:10) and children of wrath (Eph. 2:3), God loved us enough to send His Son to die in our place. Can you imagine such a thing? The Father loved the world so much, He poured out His wrath on the Son instead of those who truly deserve it. What an incredible love!

I can honestly say I love the members of our church's youth group. I would do anything to lead them to truth and see them following Christ. My heart hurts for many of them when their lives turn in harmful directions. If a gunman were to walk into our church threatening to shoot one of them, I wouldn't hesitate to take their place. I would die in the place of any one of them. I love them that much. But if a gunman walked in and forced me to choose between one of the youth or *my own son*...well, let's just say I don't love them that much. My son would come first. I have often laid this scenario out before the youth group. I have told them that if this were to ever happen, they better be prepared to meet Jesus. I would never sacrifice my own son for one of them. I love my own son much more than I love them. But

God loved us so much that He gave His Son to suffer and die.

Instead of pouring out His righteous wrath on a deserving world, He unleashed all His holy anger on His innocent Son because He loves the people who hate and revile Him. That is some kind of love. But remember that the Son was not a passive victim. Jesus freely gave Himself to be crucified and bear the Father's wrath because of His great love.

But it gets even better than that. Now, we who have been saved by Christ's death are no longer wretched and evil in the sight of the Father. Jesus took the entire weight of the Father's wrath and He gave us His perfection (2 Co. 5:21.) The New Testament repeatedly says that believers are united with Christ, co-heirs with Christ, and abide in Christ. So when the Father looks at us, He doesn't see the wretched lawbreaker. Instead, He only sees the righteousness of His Son. Can you imagine such a thing? Things that sound too good to be true are usually not true, but the gospel is an exception. Jesus gave us His perfection and we stand now perfect in the sight of the Almighty judge. No longer do believers work for righteousness. No longer do we live in fear of God's holy judgment. Those who are in Christ are free...completely free.

The evidence that the Father has accepted Jesus' sacrifice is the resurrection. Jesus was raised from the dead demonstrating that the Father has received His sacrifice and the payment for sin has been made. Through death and resurrection, Christ defeated the curse that began in the garden. Death has been vanquished. Now God has nothing but love (perfect love) for believers. I can't imagine any better news for a sinner.

Perfection has been achieved. Jesus has made us righteous before the Father. At salvation, the Holy Spirit indwells believers and begins molding them into Christ's image. We aren't perfect in our daily lives yet, but we are being perfected by the Spirit's work.

So, as we define the gospel for the purposes of examining how it affects our love for one another, we must include these facts:

1. We are utterly without goodness, absolutely wicked and evil.

2. Jesus died to pay the entire penalty for our wickedness. The Father has no more wrath for those who are in Christ.

3. Because of Jesus' life and death, the Father sees those in Christ as perfect. There is nothing they can add or take away from their standing before God

4. The proof that the Father accepted Jesus' payment is demonstrated by the resurrection. Jesus conquered sin, death, and the grave.

5. Now, Christians are being daily molded into the image of Jesus. The Holy Spirit is sanctifying believers, changing them to be in practice, what they are in position. In other words, we are righteous in God's eyes, but we are still growing in a life of righteousness.

Preaching the Gospel to Ourselves

I get criticized a lot for emphasizing the gospel's role in Christian living. It just seems too simple. When faced with the battle for holiness, people want some explanation as to why life is such a fight. The more complicated the explanation the better. People want to believe there is some secret method to the Christian life. It's just too scary to come to grips with the depths of our wickedness. Something in us refuses to accept the fact that we are helpless on our own. We know that Jesus died on the cross, but we just don't see how that helps our daily lives. Instead of thinking deeply about the gospel, we long for deeper teachings to make us better people. But still our goodness can't even move the needle on God's Holiness scale. This is why the gospel must be the focus of biblical counseling, preaching, and discipleship. If the gospel doesn't occupy this central role, all our efforts are in vain. The good news has always been the hub around which the Christian life turns.

At times, people have lost balance in their understanding, and some teachers have flat out deceived people, but throughout Church history the overarching objective of Christian counseling and proclamation was to deepen the believer's understanding of the gospel. Unfortunately in recent decades, the gospel has increasingly taken a back seat to moralistic principles. Instead of gospel preachers proclaiming the Word of God, many churches have "life coaches" teaching proper ways to behave. Instead of understanding how sanctification and spiritual growth are centered in the gospel, new and improved self-help teachings distract millions from God's authoritative message. We are given, "5 ways to a happier life," or "8 ways to improve your marriage." It's easier to follow moralistic steps and principles in order to get what we want out of life. God, Christ, the church, and the gospel become a means for getting the joy we want.

If you want principles and steps, I can give you exercises and methods that will help you act lovingly toward people. I can recommend a list of daily exercises that will help you work toward that end. We can easily focus on changing our behavior, but love will never be genuine unless it comes from a heart saturated in the gospel. Later, we will look at practical things that center our hearts upon the gospel, but first we need to understand that loving is primarily a matter of the heart. Yes, true love manifests itself in the actions it takes, but biblical love is more than that. We have already seen that bare, mechanical action is not love. Remember, Paul said he could take great actions (i.e. giving all his possessions to the poor and offering his body to be burned) but do so without love. The question of love comes down to a heart issue…and that makes it a gospel issue. The gospel is the only transformative force that can turn a heart filled with selfishness into a heart longing to sacrifice itself for Christ. There are no moralistic principles that can accomplish what only the Holy Spirit can do.

"But," you may say, "I am already saved! I already know the gospel." While that may in fact be true, this mindset, which relegates salvation to nothing more than the initial stages of the Christian life, is the problem. The salvation Jesus purchased is the whole of our Christian lives. Becoming more and more like Christ doesn't simply come by learning and applying principles. To be sure, we will continually learn and apply biblical principles as we mature and grow as Christians, but the power for internal transformation only comes by the Spirit's work of constantly revealing and applying *the gospel* in our lives. There is no deeper theological understanding, no "meatier" teaching, and no life lesson that can take the place of the powerful gospel working in our lives. Nothing else will do.

The gospel (remember our definition from above) is the framework through which we must view our world and ourselves. The price Christ paid for our sin is the lens through which we should see everything. Our greatest moments of weakness, despair, and hopelessness come when we are distracted from a gospel worldview. Allow me to illustrate the point.

When born again believers sin, the Holy Spirit convicts their hearts. If believers are not rooted and grounded in the gospel, they might quickly fall into despair thinking God has rejected them. In a sense, it is good that believers feel bad when they sin. This is the work of the Holy Spirit in their lives. We should feel bad. However, some people spiral down into defeat and despair, thinking they have ruined their standing with God and must work to regain His favor. This person has forgotten the gospel. In our own strength we are completely without goodness, even on our best day. We have no ability to earn or regain God's favor. But in Christ we are perfect, even when we sin and are convicted by the Spirit, the Father sees us in Christ. The believer's standing before God is unchanged. This is the gospel. Now we must also say that the person who reads this and thinks he is free to sin all he wants because God's grace is limitless demonstrates that he is not truly a Christian. All Christians are indwelt by the Holy Spirit and cannot practice a lifestyle of sin (1 John 3:7-10.) We cannot excuse sin because God is merciful. A believer's new heart won't allow it.

On the other hand, there are people who work their fingers to the bone thinking their labor gains them a higher position in the love of God. This person may serve constantly, evangelize relentlessly, and do all he can for the name of Christ. Of course these works are what God has called us to do. They are commanded. But the desire to work is the evidence of a changed heart. When we labor for God assuming we are earning something, we are not serving Christ. No matter how much good we do, God cannot love us more or give us a higher status in His sight. We are perfectly loved as co-heirs with Christ because of Jesus' life, death, and resurrection.

The gospel must be the center of our lives. We must never take the perfection Christ bought us for granted. We add nothing to our standing with God by working. Jesus Christ paid our debt in full. If we allow ourselves to think our good works are meriting God's love, we quickly become prideful, arrogant, and religious...like the Pharisees. Even worse, if the time comes when we can no longer accomplish mighty works for Christ, we will think our lack of performance causes God's love for us to diminish.

Many other case studies can be shown to illustrate the damage we incur when we fail to keep the gospel as our center. Without it, we will be tossed back and forth between despair and pride. However, it should now be clear that without Christ, we are completely devoid of any righteousness before the Father. Nothing we could ever do will merit anything in His eyes. But on the other hand, we are perfectly righteous in Christ and we dwell securely in the love of the Father. Nothing can diminish that love. 2 Corinthians 5:21 says, "He [the Father] made Him [the Son] who knew no sin to be sin on our behalf, so that we might become the righteousness of God in Him." Jesus took the full wrath of the Father so that we may have His perfect, unchangeable righteousness. Filtering everything through the gospel is absolutely essential as we try to love those who hurt us. But before we apply the gospel to the task of loving, we need to know why the gospel must be our focus.

You and I have enemies. Whether you know it or not, believers are caught in the middle of a war. It's a war for our hearts and minds. The world, the flesh, and the devil seek to derail your growth in Christ and destroy the effect of your service for Christ. Your enemies desire to chip away at each part of the gospel in your life.

They will tell you that you are better than the gospel says you are. They may also tell you Jesus isn't sufficient to cleanse you from all your sin. Satan would love you to think you must add your works to what Jesus did on the cross. That would be a one-way ticket to either despair or pride. If you start down that road, you can never have stability in your walk, nor a heart rooted in love. Our enemies' tactics take many forms and come in many different ways, but they always boil down to the same fundamental issue. They always deny the truth of God's word. This is the same tactic Satan tried in the Garden of Eden. He told Eve that God's word was simply not true. After God told Adam eating from the Tree of the Knowledge of Good and Evil would result in death, Satan said, "Did God really say that? No…no…no…you will not surely die. God is misleading you." Make no mistake; Satan still pushes the same lie today, it has just been neatly repackaged for a modern audience.

Because of this, we need to immerse ourselves in the gospel. We must hear it continually, study it deeply, and apply it to every situation in our lives. The gospel is not just the entry level Christian understanding. It is everything we need. But it is imperative to be reminded of this constantly. In fact, we need to preach the gospel to ourselves on a daily basis. We are utterly without righteousness, but in Christ we are perfectly righteous before God. Every day…I preach that to myself. The Apostle Paul repeatedly demonstrated this. In Paul's letter to the church at Rome, he said, "So, for my part, I am eager to preach the gospel to you also who are in Rome" (Rom. 1:15.) Paul was writing this letter to the church at Rome. Why does the church need to hear the gospel? Earlier in the epistle, Paul praised the Romans, saying that their faith in Christ was being proclaimed throughout the whole world (Rom. 1:8.) However, Paul also knew that even though the church was filled with Christians (although some may not have been truly converted), he longed to come to them and preach the gospel because they needed it. Why would Paul need to preach the gospel to believers? Modern Christians would say it's redundant to hear the gospel again and again. But Paul knew that strengthening and growing believers in the gospel is the only way they are transformed into the image of Christ.

Love and Forgiveness

Before we move into the practical aspects of loving the brethren when it hurts, we need to examine one more facet of how the gospel fortifies our love and life in the church. Jesus said it's easy to love people when they love you. Even the pagans do that (Matt. 5:46.) It's much more difficult to love those who hurt us and use us. In fact, it is impossible to love them in our own power. In order to love someone who is not very loveable (i.e. who wrongs us, annoys us, or is just mean), there must first be forgiveness. We must see past their wrongdoing and view them through a gospel-centered lens. Salvation itself must color how we see others in Christ.

Although the process of forgiving involves different things depending on the circumstances, forgiveness itself is always about releasing something. Maybe you need to let go of a past grudge or release feelings of contempt. Whatever form it takes, forgiving with our minds is much easier than forgiving with our hearts. In my mind, I have often decided to forgive someone. What a great feeling! But then I find myself remembering and replaying the circumstances that led to my hurt. I start thinking of things I wish I had said to that person. Once again, pressure starts to build as that little voice whispers, "You didn't deserve that!" Regardless of how determined I am to let it go, my heart still simmers with those feelings. Maybe I didn't do it right. I'll try letting it go again. Why does that resentment keep coming back?

When it is clear that these feelings aren't going away quietly, I just do my best to be outwardly nice to the person who offended me. Although we know it isn't true, most of us practically equate forgiveness with being nice. But is this really forgiveness? I don't think so. I may have buried the hatchet, but I left the handle sticking out of the ground.

Forgiveness is explicitly addressed in Scripture. Jesus commands His disciples to forgive those who wrong them as often as need be. He says, "Be on your guard! If your brother sins, rebuke him; and if he repents, forgive him. And if he sins against you seven times a day, and returns to you seven times, saying, 'I repent,' forgive him" (Luke 17:3-4.) Think about that for a minute. Let's say a person sins against you and says, "I'm sorry." You would probably accept their apology and move on…no big deal. But then two hours later that same person sins against you again and says, "I'm sorry." It would be a little tougher to forgive the second time, don't you think? But wait…two hours later he sins again and apologizes…then again…and again…and again. Seven times in a single day this person sins against you and apologizes. How many times could you completely forgive him and wipe away all remembrance of his wrong? After the third or fourth time, I would reach the end of my rope.

Now you are probably thinking the same thing I am. That kind of forgiveness is impossible! The disciples who heard Jesus' words also thought the same thing. The very next verse in Luke 17 records the disciples' exasperation. Luke 17:5 says, "The apostles said to the Lord, 'Increase our faith!'" They knew all too well that they could not forgive like that. A supernatural power is needed to accomplish what Jesus was commanding. The power to express this kind of forgiveness only comes from the gospel. Self-help principles won't do, and reciting religious platitudes only makes us feel worse. This kind of forgiveness only comes from the Holy Spirit.

Allow me to demonstrate what I mean. All true believers are growing in Christ. This is an unalterable fact because God promises to accomplish it. But all believers are not at the same level of sanctification. Some are more mature than others. I remember being a new Christian and thinking every aspect of my life exuded holiness. In fact, I would probably consider myself the holiest person in the room and would often wonder why Christians weren't more like me. I would think, "Why can't these people just love God like I do? Why can't they get it?" I spent many conversations bemoaning the state of Christianity and complaining about others' lack of dedication. As I think back on my entire demeanor, I'm sure I was pretty annoying to a lot of people. Of course, some people would say I am still annoying but for different reasons.

As I actually matured in Christ, I began seeing sinful things in my life that I had not recognized before. The more I understood God's holiness, the more I saw my own wretched sinfulness. Not only was I not the holiest person in the room, but I also began wondering if I had ever been holy. The more I learned about sin and righteousness, the more I understood that I am not even close to the holiness God requires. This caused despair, depression, and hopelessness because I was not grounded in the gospel of salvation.

In reality, the more I came to understand my sinfulness before God, the more I began to empathize with others' sinfulness. I already know I am utterly sinful and I know that despite my flesh, Christ saved me perfectly and gave me His righteousness. I am so thankful for God's forgiveness. Even when I do something stupid (which is quite often) and the Holy Spirit brings conviction and discipline, I still know that God's love for me hasn't changed. My standing as His child has not changed because Jesus died for my sin and gave me His perfect righteousness. As this understanding grew, I began to realize that Jesus did the same for all His people.

As believers in Christ, we are adopted into the family of God. In the Roman world (like today), the adopted child had the exact same rights and privileges as the biological heir. There is no process to "un-adopt" a son. In my own household, my son will forever be my son regardless of any action he takes. I may be disappointed in him for his actions or I may take pride in his accomplishments, but his status as my son will never change. I can be angry with him and even discipline him, but I can't make him "not" my son. Even if I were to disown him and throw him out of the house, he would still be my son. Nothing will ever change that. But in the same way, I cannot make him "more" of a son if he does great things. When he obeys and makes me proud through his accomplishments, I can't give him a higher standing in my sight. He is my son. He will always be my son. The same is true with God's children. Those who have been adopted into His family are children through the perfect blood of Christ. They can add nothing more to what they have been given, nor can they subtract from it. They may go through times of discipline when they do wrong or they may experience times of joyful fellowship as they obey, but they will always be His children.

As I have tried to make clear in this chapter, this is a matter of theology not just a matter of feeling. Sometimes I feel really bad when I fail Christ. But regardless of my feelings, I cannot undo what God's word says Christ did for me. Believing I can lose my adoption would essentially be saying Christ's death is not powerful enough to save. I would have to believe that His sacrifice was not valuable enough to pay for my sin. As a Christian, that is something I just cannot do. Christ's death and resurrection is infinitely worthy of more than I can possibly imagine. I can never affirm anything else.

On the other hand, if I were to think my works are somehow adding to my standing before the Father, I would have to affirm that Jesus' death and resurrection are not sufficient to atone for all my sin. I would have to believe that Jesus' death covered most of my sin, but there still remains sins for which His death was not sufficient. So, by adding my works, I am making up the difference that Christ failed to accomplish. Biblically, I can't accept this either. As a believer, I know Jesus paid it all and there is nothing left to do but receive the gift of salvation and walk in that truth.

Forgiving our fellow Christians involves the same theological understanding. It involves the truth of the gospel. When a believer sins against us or offends us, we shouldn't have trouble forgiving them. God doesn't have trouble forgiving them, does He? If that person is a Christian, Jesus has given perfect forgiveness. But when we refuse to forgive our brother or sister in Christ, we are essentially saying that Jesus' death is not sufficient to pay for their sin. We are saying to God, "I know your Son's death is enough to pay for their sin in *your* eyes, but the gospel is not enough for me. I require more payment than Your Son provides." Have you ever thought about forgiveness this way? Do you see how our relationship with believers has everything to do with our belief about the gospel?

Is Jesus enough to pay for the sins of all those who trust in Him? Your answer to this question is definitional to your Christianity. When we refuse to give the same forgiveness we have received, we essentially deny that Jesus is sufficient to pay for sin. We don't have a problem receiving that forgiveness for ourselves, but trusting that forgiveness for someone who has hurt us is much more difficult. Later we will examine how we practically go about administering this forgiveness, but for now we must first understand that withholding forgiveness from fellow believers who have offended us is a fundamental denial of the sufficiency of

Christ. As a Christian, I can never deny that Jesus is enough. If there is one thing of which we can be absolutely certain, it is this - the gospel is sufficient for all those who believe and it is the power of God unto salvation (Rom. 1:16.)

Chapter 5

Warning: Sheep Bite! ...and stink...and are generally annoying

In the last chapter, we drew a direct parallel between our view of the gospel and how it applies to forgiving others. As you read the previous chapter, I hope you were challenged in your belief system. Recognizing the possibility that we live inconsistently with our belief is a hard biscuit to swallow. I remember when the Spirit exposed my inconsistency in this matter. It was tough. I was faced with the fact that my confession of Christ is meaningless if Jesus is not sufficient to also forgive my brethren's sins. That kind of realization will change the way anyone thinks.

Truth be told, I act like a baby sometimes. I often respond to people with anything but love. The list of my faults would fill encyclopedias. But I can never bring myself to say that

Jesus' death is not sufficient. I was crushed when I realized that my profession of Christ is empty unless I also believe Jesus is enough to forgive others as well. Loving one another isn't just an obligation we must perform. It is a by-product of trusting in the sufficient sacrifice of the Son of God.

Once we understand that loving the brethren is gospel-centered, it becomes clear that we cannot truly love Jesus without loving His people. Jesus loves His bride. He loves her so much He gave everything for her. If we love Him, we will love what He loves. This is illustrated perfectly by Jesus' restoration of Peter in John 21:15-17. Peter confidently asserted he would never deny Christ. Yet before that night was over, he denied Jesus three times. Three people asked Peter if he was Jesus' disciple, and three times Peter denied he even knew Jesus. The man who just hours earlier promised to go to his death with Jesus, now buckled under the fear of persecution. Three times he denied his Lord.

After the resurrection, Jesus restores Peter to His service. Three times Peter is given an opportunity to re-establish his commitment. Jesus asks if Peter truly loves Him and three times Peter responds affirmatively. Then Jesus shows Peter the outworking and result of that love. Verses 15-17 say:

So when they had finished breakfast, Jesus said to Simon Peter, "Simon, son of John, do you love Me more than these?" He said to Him, "Yes, Lord; You know that I love You." He said to him, "Tend My lambs." He said to him again a second time, "Simon, son of John, do you love Me?" He said to Him, "Yes, Lord; You know that I love You." He said to him,

" Shepherd My sheep." He said to him the third time, "Simon, son of John, do you love Me?" Peter was grieved because He said to him the third time, "Do you love Me?" And he said to Him, "Lord, You know all things; You know that I love You." Jesus said to him, "Tend My sheep. (John 21:15-17.)

Jesus indicates that a true love for Him manifests in the care and nurturing of His sheep. This command is expressed in three different ways as Jesus tells Peter to tend His lambs, shepherd his sheep, and tend His sheep. We could go into detail explaining the differences between the three commands, but I think Jesus' point here is singular. The question is posed to Peter, "Do you love me?" Each time Peter affirms his love for Jesus and each time Jesus connects that love with caring for His sheep. This is also confirmed in John's first epistle when he writes, "If someone says, 'I love God,' and hates his brother, he is a liar; for the one who does not love his brother whom he has seen, cannot love God whom he has not seen (1 John 4:20.)

An authentic love for Christ will always produce an authentic love for God's people. Of course the whole point of this book is to show how that love works itself out when members of Jesus' bride are unloveable. But Jesus could not be clearer, if a person truly loves Him, that person will have a desire to love God's people – even when it is extremely difficult. Jesus' sheep can definitely be hard to love!

The Trouble With Sheep

Here in Tennessee, the scent of farmland is common. There is a particular stretch of interstate near my house that always smells of cattle. Our family has become quite used to the smell. My kids can tell you where the smell will start and where it will end as we drive down that stretch of road. Although we live in what most people consider "the country," I am not much of a country boy. I have never hunted anything and I hate the smell of farm animals. Lest you think I am a big sissy, you should know that I do love to fish and I enjoy the peacefulness of the country. Major cities hold no attraction for me at all. There are too many people and they are crammed together too closely. Yet, while my part of the country is where people raise cattle, horses, and even buffalo...farm animals are just not my thing.

The most common picture Scripture uses to speak of God's people is that of a flock of sheep. God is repeatedly called a Shepherd and His people are the sheep for whom He cares and protects. Many people have read the beauty of Psalm 23 and marveled at the picture of God bringing His people to green pastures and still waters. We can also see the comfort of knowing that Christ is the Good Shepherd who gives His life for the sheep. However, the comparison to sheep is not always a good thing. The prophet Isaiah compares God's people to sheep who have gone astray (Isa. 53:6.) Many writers and teachers have presented the characteristics of sheep and compared them to the body of Christ, and there are a host of books relating sheep-like traits to the church. Our focus here is how these traits negatively impact believers trying to love the "flock of God."

Sheep have been repeatedly characterized as stupid, but this is only partly true. Sure, compared to a dolphin or an elephant, sheep are incredibly stupid. But sheep are not really the mindless creatures they are portrayed to be. Sheep are known to recognize the face and voice of their shepherd, responding only to him. This alone presents a form of cognitive ability not found in some other animals. Regardless of what you may have been told, your goldfish doesn't recognize you.

A sheep's recognition of his shepherd is referenced when Jesus says His sheep hear His voice and will not follow a stranger (John 10:27.) But this has also been demonstrated in modern day shepherding. Even today, sheep can actually recognize and respond to the face of the shepherd who cares for them. Are sheep brilliantly clever? Not even a little bit! By any standard they are dull creatures. Therefore, I am not saying they are smart, just that they are not necessarily the mentally vacuous creatures many have claimed. So why do they act so dumb?

Sheep Follow the Flock

Granted, on a sliding scale of animal intelligence sheep are pretty dumb. But their intellect gets a bad rap for a completely different reason. Sheep have a strong flocking instinct and will not act independently of one another. For this reason, sometimes their actions make them look really stupid. For example,

Hundreds of sheep followed their leader off a cliff in eastern Turkey, plunging to their deaths while shepherds looked on in dismay. Four hundred sheep fell 15 metres to their deaths in a ravine in Van province near Iran but broke the fall of another 1,100 animals who survived. Shepherds from a nearby village neglected the flock while eating breakfast, leaving the sheep to roam free. The loss to local farmers was estimated at $74,000.[18]

Now, if I had observed this episode, I would have thought, "Wow. Sheep are really stupid!" Maybe I could understand a few members of the flock following the leader to their death...but 400? I wonder how long it took for 400 sheep to plunge to their death one by one. Then, another 1,100 jumped on top of them! On a lighter note, if you ever have trouble sleeping, you can imagine this scenario. One sheep...two sheep...

While sheep can readily recognize their shepherd, they are aimless without one. Left alone in a flock, sheep will follow the herd as it wanders haphazardly across the countryside. Their only guiding principle is "follow the leader." Where the flock moves, the individual sheep moves.

People also fall into this same mindset. Social Psychologists call it the *herd* or *mob mentality*. This disposition is seen everywhere. It causes sports fans to riot in the streets and investors to blindly follow the trends of the

---

[18] http://www.challies.com/christian-living/dumb-directionless-defenseless

stock market. Scripture also gives us many pictures of people's mob mentality. Joseph's brothers swayed Reuben to beat their younger brother and throw him in a pit. The Ephesian mob was incited against Paul by Demetrius the silversmith in Acts 19:21-41. And of course, we have the quintessential example of mob mentality in the angry crowd demanding Jesus' crucifixion before Pilate. Today, not much has changed in the way people interact with each other. Tommy Lee Jones was correct when he said, "A person is smart. People are dumb, panicky dangerous animals and you know it!"[19]

We may think herd mentality only exists where mobs act in violent aggression, but people are disposed to follow the crowd in all kinds of ways. Wherever people assemble in any size social groups, a herd mindset presents itself. Even those individuals who choose not to fellowship with the congregation take part in this flocking mindset. The herd mentality doesn't just materialize when mobs of people scream at each other. Because people are social animals, we don't want to be viewed as "out of the crowd." Even when we don't actively socialize with one another, we don't want people to think ill of us.

The most amazing thing about this phenomenon is that it only takes one or two people to turn an entire crowd in an unhealthy direction. Now, if your congregation bursts into a violent mob, threatening to lynch you...there are probably

---

[19] Yes. As a matter of fact I did just quote agent Kay from *Men in Black*.

bigger issues at stake than what we are addressing here. My advice to you would be to find a different place to worship. Most often, this mindset manifests itself when one or two people spread gossip or speak negatively about someone in the congregation. Maybe you have experienced something like this in the past. Once damaging words are spoken, they cannot ever be retracted. Even when the person who committed this sin repents and apologizes, the herd mentality causes the flock to always look for the negative in you. The remembrance of what was said remains. The accusation will always be in the minds of people as they interact and assemble with you. A single person's loose tongue can easily put you on the defensive as you fight what feels like a losing battle. When something is thought to be "common knowledge" among the crowd, it doesn't matter if it is true or not. The question will always be in the back of people's minds.

This phenomenon is quite common in the secular world, but many of us don't expect to find it in the church. Christians are supposed to be righteous people aren't they? But we have already seen that believers (in themselves) aren't righteous at all. Of course, Christ allows tares to grow up with the wheat (Matt. 13:24-30), and we should always be aware that not every person who claims to be a Christian actually follows Christ. But true disciples aren't righteous either. If we understand the gospel, we don't need to wonder why people get hurt in church. The Bible says we are all wretched and sinful. It should come as no shock when people's sin affects us in harmful ways.

Understanding this, the obvious question is, "How do we deal with it?" Keeping our eyes on the Shepherd prevents us from wandering into dangerous territory, but what should we do when other sheep wound us? How do we love people when faced with this kind of abuse? We will get to that later. Right now we must make sure we understand that though we are called God's sheep, the flock is not practically pure as the driven snow. Without keeping their eyes fixed on the Shepherd, sheep will always wander wherever the flock takes them.[20] Well-meaning people are often swept up into the controversies and gossip of the crowd. If it hasn't happened to you yet, it will. Eventually you will be caught in the undertow of such bleating.

Sheep Are Udderly Defenseless[21]

Sheep cannot protect themselves from anything. Almost every other animal has some sort of defensive mechanism. When injured or backed into a corner, some animals can fight. Other animals have the speed to simply run away. Sheep have neither of these capabilities. They can and do run away from danger, but any predator worth its fangs can easily catch a sheep. The only defense sheep have is the flock and the shepherd.

When a predator attacks a flock of sheep, they band

---

[20] This includes "flocks" wandering into doctrinal heresy, secularism, or liberal viewpoints. Although not the main focus of this book, sheep without a shepherd invariably find themselves wandering away from the Christian faith itself!

[21] "Udderly" – Udders…get it? Female sheep have udders…Oh nevermind.

together and run around in circles. Their means of protecting themselves is to simply cause confusion and hope the predator grabs someone else. Oh I could draw so many parallels with the modern church here! It reminds me of the old joke where two hikers try to run from a bear. One stops to put on his tennis shoes. The other hiker says, "You can't outrun the bear even with running shoes." The shoed hiker explains that he doesn't have to outrun the bear. He just has to outrun the other hiker. Sheep don't have a credible defense against anything. When the enemy comes, the best they can do is move out of the way and let him take their buddy. If that doesn't sound like church people's actions, I don't know what does!

People feel better when someone else is the object of scorn and ridicule. Just like sheep, people want to be part of the flock and feel more secure when they are in close proximity to it. And just like sheep, the only defense people have against the enemy is to flock together and turn to the Shepherd. United, the Church of Jesus is a force to be reckoned with. Jesus Himself said the gates of hell would never prevail against His church. Unfortunately, many don't recognize that the only thing ensuring the church's victory is their unity with the Shepherd who guides it. Later, we will see that there is indeed protection from spiritual enemies among the fellowship of believers, but many don't desire this true protection. The protection of the Shepherd always manifests itself in the presentation of truth, and God's truth necessitates a heart of repentance and humility. There is true protection in submitting to Him, but we have already seen how difficult it is for man to humble himself. Many refuse to conform to God's holiness, assuming that being "in the crowd" protects them. As we have earlier seen, the gospel proclaims our inability and immorality. Realizing we are vulnerable and powerless outside of Christ drives some people to safeguard themselves by pushing someone else into the enemy's crosshairs. The flock bands together as it pushes a hapless sacrifice outside for the predator.

Lest we become unbalanced, we must also understand that flocking together is a good thing. Believers are called to invest themselves in the assembly and bear one another's burdens. We are supposed to be united together! But the only defense we have against the world, the flesh, and the devil is the protection of the Shepherd. When the sheep reject the instruction and correction of the Shepherd, there is no safety. All believers must remember this. We can't do anything about those sheep who throw us under the bus, hoping to keep themselves from being voted off the island. But we can seek the comfort and protection of the Shepherd when the sheep begin biting each other.

Sheep Stink

O.K. This might just be my particular sensitivity to smelliness. Strangely enough, I have met people who love the smell of barnyard animals. I don't understand it, but to each his own. Even if you do enjoy the subtle aroma of musty manure, you have to admit that sheep smell worse than many other animals.

Sheep naturally produce an oily wax called lanolin.

Sometimes people call it wool fat or wool wax. Sebaceous glands in the skin produce the lanolin which waterproofs, hydrates, and lubricates the sheep's wool and skin. Lanolin is stripped from the wool when it is sheared from the sheep, and there is a great market for the substance in the form of cosmetic products and lubricants. But everyone who has come into contact with sheep can attest to lanolin's most pervading quality. It stinks! The word "stink" doesn't really capture the magnitude of the smell. The people who regularly work with unprocessed wool can't get the smell out of their hands. Woolly sheep covered in lanolin smell with a gamey, musty, damp, funk that no adjective can accurately describe.

And because of the consistency of this oily compound, their wool picks up every piece of dirt they rub up against. Picture an oily sponge being dropped into the dirt. That's what a sheep romping through the countryside looks like. When you see the word "sheep," you get a picture of a snow-white lamb that smells like laundry detergent. That is most certainly not what sheep are like. Their wool is never pure white. In fact, a pile of recently sheared wool is one of the nastiest things I have ever seen. A full sized ewe will yield a fleece between eight and twelve pounds, but thirty to forty percent of that weight is dirt, vegetable matter, and lanolin. Everything clings to their wool. Grass, dirt, and twigs are always stuck in the matted coat. Some farmers will disagree with me, but in my opinion, sheep are the nastiest of creatures.

People also tend to collect the garbage that's around

them. It sticks to us like dirt on a sheep. I may be revealing my own inadequacy and sin here, but when I get lazy in my fellowship with the brethren and my dependence upon Christ, I always catch myself slipping back into worldliness. When I neglect my dependence upon God and His people, I am far more likely to fall into the snare of temptation and listen to the lies of the enemy. The world's garbage clings to me and weighs me down. As I fellowship with the brethren, iron truly sharpens iron and God uses them to convict and instruct me. When I place myself under the preaching of God's Word, He illuminates my path and reveals the necessity of following hard after Him. Investing myself in prayer empowers me to live for Him in the face of trial and circumstance. But when those disciplines are neglected, my fleece collects mounds of smelly grime. In my own life, I have noticed a pattern. Neglecting God's Word and His people always leads to increased temptation and worldliness.

The fruits of the Spirit are forced to grow when I fellowship with the saints. For example, Christ is growing my patience when someone tests that patience. Therefore, when I invest my life in church people, God is shearing away the grime that has accumulated on me. Independence from the flock always produces selfishness and pride. As the Spirit applies the preached Word to my personal circumstances in the community of faith, God is shearing away the filth I have walked through in my daily life. An illustration that demonstrates this reality occurs as Jesus washes the disciples' feet in John 13. Jesus girds himself with a towel and begins doing the task only a menial servant would do. He washes the disciples' nasty feet. Of course the outspoken Peter protests when Christ comes to his feet. Jesus tells Peter, "If I do not wash you, you have no part with Me" (John 13:8.) This prompts Peter to concede, but he tells Jesus not just to wash his feet. He wants Jesus to wash his whole body. Jesus answers him saying, "He who has bathed needs only to wash his feet, but is completely clean" (John 13:10.)

Remember that no one sported tennis shoes in the first century. Everyone wore sandals, and to get from one place to another, people had to walk on dirty roads. As they walked through the world, dirt and grime gathered on their feet. Jesus assures Peter that he is perfectly clean because he has trusted in the word of God. Yet, Peter had to walk through the road's dust in order to reach the upper room. His feet collected the dirt of the road. In the same way, believers are clean. Jesus has given His perfect righteousness and made us spotless before a Holy God. But as we walk through this fallen world, the grime of the road collects on our feet.

So many people don't understand this. They don't see a need to submit themselves to a local body and serve. It doesn't seem necessary to continually hear the gospel preached and see the fruits of the Spirit grow as believers serve each other. Then, the person who continually neglects the church wakes up one day and can't understand why they are spiritually dry. They can't understand how they have strayed so far away from the Shepherd. The grime of the world that has collected on them obscured their view of

Christ.

There are two sides to this story. Grime collects on others in the same way it does on you. Sometimes that worldly filth shows itself in the conflict and antagonism believers experience. We have already seen this fact. Christ has called us to be transformed by the renewing of our minds (Rom. 12:2.) When we refuse to submit our minds to the reality of God's Word and submit our bodies as living sacrifices, our minds are not renewed. Instead, we quickly find ourselves quickly conformed to this world.

Sheep Bite

In reality, most sheep won't bite you. More likely, a sheep will butt you with its head. Personally, I would rather be bitten than head butted. Regardless of the tactic, the point is the same. Sometimes these kind-hearted, fluffy, mild-mannered sheep can hurt you!

Let's face facts. Christ's sheep can be hurtful and very often bite the hand trying to feed them. His sheep are sinners by nature and all too often they are selfish and mean. But Jesus said if we truly loved Him, we would tend His sheep. This means we will care for them, exhort them, and be there to shepherd them through difficult times. This idea of church fellowship is declining rapidly in American churches. Instead of gathering with the brethren to exhort one another and worship God together, many in our increasingly individualistic society are coming to the church to receive instead of give. The church is quickly becoming a nameless faceless organization providing for people's material needs.

Of course the body of Christ does provide for hurting people, but the church is not nameless, nor is it faceless. The church is made up of the people who fellowship together and are united together in Christ.

Vast amounts of people have left churches feeling they weren't being properly cared for. But many of these same people have never lifted a finger to help others in their fellowship. I once received a phone call from a gentleman who complained that no one bothered to come visit him during his stay in the hospital. Hospital visitation is a very important part of ministry and normally this would concern me a great deal. But this situation was different. This individual did not fellowship at our church. He slipped in the back door after service started and slipped out before the service was finished. He never even associated with anyone in the church. A few people knew him, but he was not in any small group, Bible study, or Sunday school class. The majority of the members didn't even know his name, yet here he was chastising me because no one visited him.

I don't do well in situations like that. When people are selfish and presumptuous, I have an extremely hard time loving them. As I write these words, I literally feel the weight of my failure to love him like Christ. I started my answer well by simply apologizing to the man. But, then I feigned outrage that church people would neglect such a task and asked him to give me a list of all the people he visited in the hospital. I told him I would confront them and demand to know why they did not return the love he had shown them. In addition to this, I asked which Sunday school class he attended so I could go chastise them for not visiting one of their faithful classmates. Needless to say, he couldn't name a single person he had visited in the hospital, nor could he tell me which class he attended. We both knew he hadn't attended any class. He quickly realized I was being insultingly sarcastic but the point was made. He expected everyone else to do the task of "tending to the sheep" although he had been habitually unwilling to do the same.

It is easy for me to show you all the faults in the man. I could also show you a vast multitude of people who treat the church the same way, but the real point is about me. Why is it so hard for me to love him as one of Christ's sheep? To this day, I still don't know what I should have said. What would Christ have said? Christians who love Christ (there is no other kind) should be those who care for the sheep of Christ, even if we doubt that an individual is truly Christ's. Believers are those who love God's lambs and tend to them rather than attempt to get what they can from them. Believers should not be like the man in this story who had absolutely nothing to do with the sheep. They certainly shouldn't expect the sheep to treat them with love and care if they have offered none. But neither should Christians be like the sarcastic pastor who tried to do nothing more than prove a point. Neither of these exhibits the mind of Christ.

Clearly, Christ's sheep are selfish and can be very hurtful. In this case, the un-invested man and the smart aleck pastor were selfish. But we could list so many more examples. If you follow a group of sheep long enough, eventually you will get poo on your shoes. But even then, believers should love those who have not yet matured to the point of selflessness among the brethren. In this case, I was not tending to this man as one of Christ's sheep. Rather than giving him an ironic reprimand (regardless of how clever it was,) I should have loved and tended to him as Christ commanded. Jesus may have taken the opportunity to grow this man if I would have demonstrated His love and compassion.

News Flash: It's Not About You

It's wonderful to extol the merits of Christ's love and tell everyone what we are supposed to do. So far that's all I have done in this chapter. I'm sure most of you reading this know the proper, loving way believers are commanded to respond when people use us. In fact, if I were to simply write out a list of situations and the proper Christian response to those situations, it would quickly turn into nothing more than platitudes and moralistic stock phrases. Nothing I have said is new. We all know these things. The truth is that Christ's sheep bite and when they bite, it hurts. As long as Jesus is in the business of saving sinners, this won't change. God's people aren't good people. They are wretched sinners saved by undeserved grace and God knows exactly what He is doing by putting different types of people together. He is using them to grow one another. No matter what congregation or fellowship you attend, God will always place people there to help sanctify you (and some do a better job than others.) Most of the time, this sanctification means they get on your last nerve and you must learn patience and long-suffering.

Before we move into what tending Christ's sheep actually means, we must also readily admit that not everyone attending church is part of God's family. The church (the true church) is not going to hell in a hand basket, regardless of what the Sunday morning church crowd looks like. God's people are still seeking after God, loving each other, and worshiping their Lord. They are walking humbly with their God and growing in the fruits of the Spirit. But we would be very naïve if we didn't recognize that whenever there are genuine believers present, there are also counterfeits. One of the unfortunate problems in the visible church is the growing rate of false converts, especially among young people. So I am not saying that every person you come in contact with is an authentic Christian growing in Christ.

Likewise, we cannot sacrifice the truth of the gospel for the sake of loving someone. We cannot throw doctrine out the window and embrace unbiblical views as we try to "all just get along." There are definite reasons to break fellowship with people and reasons for church discipline. But we will examine these things in depth later. For now, as we look at loving, tending, and shepherding Christ's sheep, we are assuming that those with whom we have contact are truly Christ's sheep. The question here is, "How do we deal with Christians when they offend or annoy us? How do we love them and shepherd them as we are commanded when everything inside us wants to run the other way?" Make no mistake, loving Jesus' bride hurts.

Many people in the church grew up as part of a local fellowship. Because of this, many think that strife, conflict, and selfishness are simply the way churches operate. Anyone who has been an invested part of a local church can tell you stories of heated exchanges during business meetings, rumors being thrown around haphazardly, or entire portions of the congregation splitting off to become a separate church. Although, we inherently know these things should not be, we have accepted them as inevitable. On the other hand, un-churched people are shocked when they see such discord. Understandably, many become disenfranchised when the church exhibits the same behaviors they have seen so often in the world. Many people choose to simply disconnect themselves from the fellowship. Dealing with people is too difficult. It is common for some believers to think their absence from the congregation won't make a difference. They assume agents of change among the brethren are only those with special gifts and talents. Only influential or eloquent people can be used of God in the body. They believe only someone more holy than they can tend Christ's sheep.

The Body

A flock of sheep is not the only metaphor Scripture uses to describe God's people. On more than one occasion, Paul uses the figure of the body to describe the church. In 1 Corinthians 12, Paul describes believers as part of Christ's body. Before we look at what Paul says, consider your own body for a moment. I'll bet you value every part of your body. You may dislike the shape of your thighs or the size of your stomach, but you surely don't dislike them enough to remove them. Your eyes may not work like they used to, but even blind people don't remove their eyes. When you remove a part of your body it immediately starts dying. In the same way body parts can't function when removed from the body, there are no "lone ranger" Christians. Believers cannot grow spiritually outside of the fellowship any more than your hand would continue to grow if it were severed from your arm. Just the opposite is true. The moment your hand separates from your body it starts dying and a believer separated from the body will spiritually wither.

A friend of mine had an infection set up in his big toe. Although the doctors treated him with antibiotics and various other medications, the prognosis was most likely amputation. I myself have never faced such a decision, but I remember thinking, "Man, just cut it off. It's only a toe." Of course it didn't make a big difference to me, it wasn't *my* toe. My friend didn't want to lose a part of his body and when he was forced to do so, he quickly discovered that he couldn't walk the same without it. Even the body parts we take for granted are necessary and useful. I must admit that this illustration isn't perfect. Many people have their tonsils or appendixes removed and never miss them in the slightest. But in the day Paul wrote these words, there were no such practices. No one was cutting away body parts. Even today, no one wants to lose a hand or a foot. People don't want to lose an ear even though it wouldn't necessarily affect their hearing. Our bodies are precious to us. Each part performs a specific function and, even if a part fails in its duty, we don't readily want it removed.

Even if we are talking about a body part that continually gives you trouble, you probably want to keep it. A hand may be infected and present a real danger of spreading throughout the body, but no one wants it removed unless it is absolutely necessary. In the same way, Paul tells the Corinthians that every member of the church (every true member) is valuable and absolutely necessary. While the analogy of severing a part from the body isn't perfect, the principle it teaches is singularly irrefutable. Every born again believer is needed in the local fellowship. Everyone has a gift to offer and everyone has a role. No one is a malfunctioning appendix. Every believer serves a purpose...even those whose only job is to grow our patience. It may not be that pleasant, but God uses them too. We are all part of the body and we must care for each other accordingly.

Paul makes two astounding claims as he describes the parts of the body. First, he teaches that no one can say he or she is not valuable to the body and thereby separate themselves from it. Paul says, "If the foot says, 'Because I am not a hand, I am not a part of the body,' it is not for this reason any the less a part of the body. And if the ear says, 'Because I am not an eye, I am not a part of the body,' it is not for this reason any the less a part of the body?" (1 Co. 12:15-16.) Paul's point is that no believer can say he is not needed in the body. The foot cannot say he is unnecessary because he is not used as a hand. He cannot separate himself from the body because of his perception. Likewise, the ear cannot refuse to be part of the body because he is not used for seeing. Each individual is placed in the body for a specific purpose and given a specific gift. No person has the right to exempt himself from the body because he feels he is not needed. Every part of the body is needed, even if you don't completely understand how you are being used.

Paul continues his argument by saying, "And the eye cannot say to the hand, 'I have no need of you'; or again the head to the feet, 'I have no need of you.' On the contrary, it is much truer that the members of the body which seem to be weaker are necessary" (1 Co. 12:21-22.) The "important" parts of the body, which are members who seem to be the most gifted and useful, must never think other members are somehow less important. All parts are needed because God has placed them in the body and given them gifts to use. It may not be a gift that is extravagantly noticeable by the entire congregation, but that does not change its importance.

In addition to this, God puts people in the fellowship to learn and grow from other believers. When a person thinks he is so important to the body that he can accomplish the mission himself, he is treading very dangerous ground. No Christian, regardless of how much he has been gifted, can look at a brother or sister and say, "The body doesn't need you." The eye cannot say it does not need the ear. Indeed, Paul culminates his teaching about the body by saying, "so that there may be *no division* in the body, but that the members may have the same *care for one another*. And if one member suffers, *all the members suffer with it*; if one member is honored, all the members rejoice with it" (1 Co. 13:25-26.)

Every true believer is needed and every believer is to be part of the fellowship. Lone Ranger Christians are living in direct disobedience to the word of God. Just like some members are eyes and used for seeing, some members are hands and used for grasping. The real issue comes when we begin to recognize that some church members act like the *rear end* of the body. Sometimes it may seem like they are just there to make the rest of the body smell funny. Without going into graphic illustrations, it should suffice to say that even these members of the body are necessary. Even they are being sanctified and growing in the Spirit.

Growing Pains

I am a pretty hardheaded guy. If you don't believe me, you should ask my wife...my parents...my friends...and pretty much anyone else who knows me. I have come to realize that the most significant lessons God has taught me stem from adversity, trial, and difficulty. Rarely do I learn hard life lessons on the first try. Usually, I think I can handle things myself. Because of this, God has to forcefully get my attention when He wants to teach me something. I am also a bookworm. If I want to learn something, I just go find a book written by an expert and learn how to do it. Just give me the facts, the procedure, the inner workings, and I'll be fine. This is how I usually approach theology as well, but when God wants to actually teach me something, He usually has to humble me so I can actually experience it. I can learn facts from reading, but performing them usually takes a much harder lesson.

It's like learning to ride a bicycle. As a parent, you can explain all the mechanics of bike riding to your child. You may take great pains demonstrating how to shift your weight and pedal in a continuous motion in order to maintain balance and forward movement. The child could read books that explain everything there is to know about bike riding. This would surely provide the child with an abundance of useful information, but until the child actually gets out on that bike and crashes a few times, he or she will never actually learn to ride a bike.

God works the same way with me. I can study about love and understand all the relevant principles regarding patience and kindness. I know all too well how I should react to situations, but until I actually put that patience into practice, I don't truly know how to be patient. This usually means I fail at being patient a few times before I understand what patience is. Until I am forced to be kind when kindness is not my natural reaction, I really don't understand kindness. I can give you the definition of kindness, but actually being kind is different. This is how God grows the fruits of the Spirit in me. As a child, I memorized the fruits of the Spirit in Sunday School. I can still recite them: love, joy, peace, patience, kindness, goodness, faithfulness, gentleness, and self-control. Even as I wrote them out just now, the song that helped me memorize them ran through my head. But simply knowing them doesn't really help me practice them. Knowing these are the products of the Holy Spirit doesn't cause me to be more gentle or kind. But when God throws some selfish annoying church member in my path, I finally realize what being patient and long-suffering truly means...*because I don't naturally exhibit those qualities.* When my patience is tested, I am shown the mirror of God's command in order to see how defective my patience is.

To be perfectly honest, this entire book came about because of my lack of patience, kindness, long-suffering, etc. The more I deal with church folks, the more I realize how sinful I really am and how much I need the Spirit's help to grow. That is why one of my favorite verses is Romans 8:28, "And we know that God causes all things to work together for good to those who love God, to those who are called according to His purpose." This means that all the difficulties and the tiresome experiences I have with unaccommodating people are part of God's plan for my good (and theirs too.) Just like a child can't learn to ride a bike without falling on his face, we can't grow in patience unless that patience is tested. We also can't grow in love unless we are continuously put in situations when it is difficult to love.

All this sounds suspiciously like I am saying that church people attack for your own good. I'm sure that doesn't help much, but our aim as disciples of Christ is to be conformed to His image rather than just be comfortable. We are sinfully wicked people who still dwell with the flesh that desires its own good. Although the Holy Spirit now indwells us and produces a supernatural desire to love, our flesh still battles against it. This condition is true in every believer. We might look around and see people we think are much holier than we (and indeed they may be), but we can never forget that even those we hold in high regard struggle against their flesh just as we do.

The struggle against the flesh is played out on the stage of life, which means, when God's Word breaks forth in your heart and you understand the necessity of love, simple acknowledgment is not sufficient to sanctify you. You must actually learn how to practice love. Since it is easy to love people who love you in return, the only way selfless love grows is in the fertile soil of opposition. We need a fresh supply of people who are hard to love so we can learn to love like Jesus. When love doesn't come easy, we must learn to depend on Christ for it. Trial brings greater manifestations of the fruits of the Spirit. James tells us to, "Consider it all joy, my brethren, when you encounter various trials, knowing that the testing of your faith produces endurance [patience]. And let endurance [patience] have its perfect result, so that you may be perfect and complete, lacking in nothing" (James 1:2-4).

Earlier, I mentioned that I worked as an auto body repair tech for quite some time. I started doing bodywork by accident. The owner of a local body shop needed some temporary help and I needed some money. When I started, I didn't know anything about bodywork. I had to learn. Because reading is the primary way I learn facts and information, I just got a textbook about auto bodywork and found some information about certification. Before long, I was studying to take the ASE certification tests. These tests certify that automotive mechanics and repair techs are competent and capable to do the work. Large-scale body shops require their employees to be ASE certified. Since I am pretty good at retaining facts and information, and I have always been good at taking standardized tests...can you guess what happened? I passed all five tests with flying colors. I passed the test centered on painting and bodywork. I passed the test on repairing automotive suspensions and restoring wrecked frames. I even passed electrical portions of those tests. Yet, even though I was now a completely certified auto body technician – I didn't know a thing about any of the stuff I was certified in! I have painted cars and dabbled in repairing frames but when it came time to actually do serious bodywork, I wasn't able. Imagine this guy walking into your place of business with all these certifications only to find out he didn't know how to do anything he was certified to do. That was me! Fortunately, I had bosses that were willing to work with me and teach me. But the reality hit home with a thunderous explosion of failure and embarrassment. Until I actually start practicing these skills on an increasingly more difficult level, I will never get any better at it. I can read all the books about bodywork I want, but if I can't lay my hands on a frame and pull it into position, I can't do the work.

Reading a book about God's Word isn't the same as digesting God's Word, which is itself powerful and transformative. But neither can we simply internalize the biblical principles of love and expect no challenges in the practice of them. Until someone comes along who tests your patience, your patience won't grow. Until someone un-loveable invades your space, your love for people won't grow. There is no reason for love to grow until you meet someone you can't love. Learning to love people in spite of their sin is not quick and easy. If you were expecting a book telling you the "secret" that transforms you into a person who loves like Christ in every situation...I'm sorry. I wish there were such a thing, I really do. But Scripture does tell us how this transformation comes about. Growing in the fruits of the Spirit occurs as the Word of God renews our minds and the struggles of life put our renewed minds into practice. The old hymn rings with unbearable truth when it says, "Trust and obey – for there's no other way – to be happy in Jesus – than to trust and obey."

Chapter 6

Love is A Battlefield

Well Hello! After the last few paragraphs, I am glad you are still reading. When some people realize that the Christian life is a desperate struggle, many lose interest. The relentless intensity of the struggle is overwhelming and quite frankly too exhausting for the natural man. The whole endeavor seems incredibly difficult especially since we all lead such busy lives. It's much easier not to worry about loving other people. Disconnecting from people we don't like is much simpler, but that is devastating to our Christian lives. Nothing dismantles our growth faster than removing ourselves from the fellowship of the saints. So many believers seek counseling when they feel spiritually dry. They don't like feeling stagnant in their relationship with Christ. But one of the most important things for growth, the fellowship of the saints, is the one thing they refuse to invest in. Please don't misunderstand me. I think Christians really want to grow. A believer's heartfelt desire is to fellowship with the saints, but as we have said before, placing oneself in a position to potentially be hurt by other people is hard. It's especially hard when you have repeatedly been hurt in the past. So what are we supposed to do? If we truly desire to love like Jesus, how do we begin?

First, let us summarize what we have learned. Love is not just an emotional feeling in your heart. Our hearts are deceitful and naturally selfish so it's easy for us to mistake infatuation, desire, or compassion for true love. But remember, love isn't just raw actions either. People can easily perform actions that appear loving while having hearts filled with selfish motivations. Likewise, it's common for people to carry out loving actions with anger or resentment. True love and heartfelt compassion are always demonstrated in selfless action, but one cannot exist without the other. Action without emotion is empty. Yet, emotion without action is a charade. Paul describes Christian love as "esteeming others better than ourselves" (Phil. 2:3.) Biblical love involves both emotion and activity, and we have already seen that transforming our hearts is something only God accomplishes. Christ is continually molding our hearts as we are compelled to love those who are difficult to love. This shows us the limitations and failings of our love, but it also forces us to depend on Christ for our lack of love.

Scripture so often commands believers to love the brethren that no serious student of the Bible can deny it.

But this Christ-like love is not demonstrated in our love for our parents, children, or close friends. Jesus said even pagans and sinners do that. Christ's love is seen when we love those who do not reciprocate that love.

Unfortunately, we are also forced to admit that there is no magic bullet that automatically makes us love like Christ. Although we may find many books and sermons claiming to provide the secret to loving others, there is no ancient church secret which has been lost to modern Christians. Neither is there some secret knowledge or mystical understanding that has eluded Christians for two thousand years. Believers have long known that Christ's command to love is impossible for the natural man. Grasping this concept is extremely unnerving for believers who desperately desire to follow Christ's mandate. The disciples themselves were distressed when faced with their inability to love (Luke 17:3-5.) But the only way we grow to love like Christ is to grow in our relationship with Christ. There is no quick and easy way to accomplish this. God sanctifies us through a lifetime of being transformed by God's word and through the people who test the limits of our love.

This is a point we must firmly grasp. God grows us in our love by showing us the boundaries of our love. God develops our love by sending people who push the limits of our love. When we fail to love like Christ, the Spirit convicts us and we grow. Think of this process like the stretching of a rubber band. Let's say a small rubber band represents the way we love. God wants our rubber band to be huge like Christ's. If God were to simply stretch the rubber band until it matched Christ's, it would break. So he gently stretches the rubber band a little at a time, but He always stretches it slightly past its capability. When He releases the rubber band it goes back to a relaxed shape but it is a little bit bigger than it was before. Its elasticity has been stretched. Then it gets stretched again, far beyond what it is able. But when it relaxes it is once again bigger than it was before. This is how God grows our love. Every time our love is stretched and we fail to love like we should, it snaps back bigger than before. When we fail to love someone, our deficiency spurs us to improve. The Holy Spirit shows us what we should have done. In this way, our love grows...slowly but surely. It rarely happens as fast as we want, but it is happening. Christ promised it would happen.

Do You Really Want It?

But the question is, "Do you really want to love the unloveable?" Everyone sacrifices for what they want...everyone. No obstacle will stand in our way if we truly want something. We will sacrifice time, energy, and money for anything we consider valuable. Some people refuse to waste time reading books, but will jump at the chance to go watch a sports team. Others don't want to spend money for tickets to the big game, but have no problem shelling out the same money for a night of fine dining. Many husbands have said they cannot afford new jewelry for the wife, but suddenly come home with a new bass boat. We will always find a way to get what we love. Even Jesus said, "Where your treasure is, your heart would be there also."

The Senior Pastor where I serve tells a story about a man asking for prayer to help him quit smoking. He smoked for many years and desperately wanted to kick the habit. In the midst of an otherwise ordinary conversation, the man asked this pastor to pray that God would help him give up cigarettes. The pastor energetically said he would pray for the man. In fact, he asked the man if he wanted to pray about it immediately. The smoker agreed. So they got down on their knees to pray. Before they even closed their eyes, the pastor told the man how he intended to pray. He said, "I know you really want to quit smoking so I am going to pray that if you ever put another cigarette in your mouth, God would strike you dead on the spot!" Before the pastor could say another word, the man jumped to his feet and refused to pray. He wanted to quit, but he wasn't fully committed to quitting. In reality, he didn't want to quit at all. He knew that smoking was bad for him and eventually would take its toll on his body. He also knew that the best thing for him would be to lay the cigarettes down and never touch them again. But he wasn't ready to sacrifice anything in order to quit. He wasn't truly desperate about quitting yet. He would have been happy to pray for the Lord take away the desire to smoke. He would love praying to receive strength to quit. However, he wasn't ready to bet his life on it. In his heart, he knew that he really loved smoking. There may come a day when his health is more important to him than smoking, (perhaps when the doctor diagnoses him with a disease) but that day hadn't arrived yet.

So many of us are the same way about growing in Christ. We desire to grow in our love, but we just aren't ready to give anything up for it yet. I may truly desire to lose weight, but until I am ready to sacrifice the gooey goodness of sugary sweets, I don't *really* want to lose weight. In my mind I certainly wish I were thinner, but that desire is not yet more powerful than my craving for food.

Becoming more like Christ is similar to this in so many people's lives. We mentally want to be more like him. We really do. All born again believers desire to be like Christ,[22] but too many of us are not willing to sacrifice for it. We are not ready to leave the entertainment of the world or the comforts we enjoy in order to grow in Christ. We are not willing to give up free time in order to spend time in focused prayer or reflective Bible study. It's easy to say we want to love the brethren like Christ does, but we are deceiving ourselves if we are unwilling to sacrifice the "me-centered"

---

[22] Ezekiel 36:26-27 tells us God Himself accomplishes this in His children. We still fail and sin repeatedly, but God promises to give us a heart desiring to obey Him.

practices that make loving others so difficult. Please don't misunderstand me. I am not just giving you another rule – "stop being so sinful and love people." If loving people were that easy, we wouldn't need a whole book about it. I am saying that although we will have to fight against our selfish inclinations as we become more and more like Christ – we should be *willing* to do whatever it takes to be conformed to His image.

Since we will always find a way to overcome obstacles in order to obtain what we truly desire, cultivating a desire to love like Jesus is what must change. If we truly desire to love like Christ, we will fight for it. At this moment, you may not be loving others very well. If you can freely admit that, I want to welcome you to the club. We have ID cards and everything. But, as a born again believer, you should have a heartfelt desire to love the church like Jesus does. Loving others is definitely hard, and church folks don't make it easy, but if the inner desire is not there you should rightfully question your relationship with Jesus.

That being said, you must understand that this is a call to war. As Christians, the flesh is our enemy. Yes, the devil is also our enemy but the only stronghold the devil has in our lives is our flesh and our sin. Our own sinful hearts are fighting against us as the indwelling Spirit molds us into the image of Jesus. The picture of the Christian life is not one of tranquility, as we lay on a beach being fanned with palm leaves. Rather, the Christian life is a picture of a soldier on high alert, wading through the jungle as he seeks out the enemy he is tasked to destroy. If you dropped a soldier in the middle of a war zone, it would be ridiculous to think his attitude would be one of complacency and satisfaction. More likely, all his senses would be pointed toward what he truly desires – to survive and complete his mission. Is this how we think? Are all our senses focused on battling the flesh, which continually tempts us toward selfishness? When a brother or sister wrongs us, are we immediately alerted to the fact that it's our sinful flesh calling us to retaliation? The Holy Spirit guides us to love and forgive, but the flesh is much easier to follow. Resisting temptation and following Jesus' example is a fight! It's a war. Are you ready to enlist in the fight or would you rather relax and be tossed wherever your emotions take you? How you answer this question determines how you will grow in your love.

Fighting the Flesh

Finally we come to the real question. Do you want to love like Christ? If the answer is yes, then you must fight for it. The ability to love the un-loveable will never fall out of the sky. This love won't passively come upon you when you least expect it. It comes through blood, sweat, and tears. It comes by fighting against the sinful part of us that desires to have it's own way. Our love only grows as we recognize our failures, trust in the gospel, and fight against our flesh.

The flesh is always "me-centered." That sinfulness rises up whenever we feel wronged or disrespected. In these moments, we are locked in a battle between the flesh and Spirit. We battle from a position of victory in the gospel, but there is a battle nonetheless. Jesus has already won the battle we are fighting. We are perfect in Christ and nothing can ever change that. The Father looks at believers through the blood of Christ...and through Christ, He sees perfection. From this victory, we are called to assault our flesh as we strive to obtain in practice what we have been given in position. When you picked up this book, you were probably expecting some profound teaching that would make loving others easy. I'm sorry to disappoint you, but there is no such thing. Jesus' love fills those who trust in Him, but our flesh continually besieges that love. If you want to love what Jesus loves, you must fight for it.

We see a perfect picture of this mindset in Jacob's wrestling match with God. In Genesis 32, Jacob formulated a plan to appease the wrath of his brother Esau, whom he had wronged. As Jacob prepared to meet his brother, he was afraid of what would happen. That night, God appeared to Jacob. At the time, Jacob didn't know it was God. Jacob thought a man was attacking him. The two men wrestled all night. The Bible simply says, "a man wrestled with him until daybreak." Don't pass over this tiny sentence without feeling the weight of it. If you have ever been in a fight or a wrestling match, you know that it takes a great deal of energy to wrestle all night long. I can imagine the men sweating, pulling at each other, falling on the ground, and rolling around trying to get the upper hand. Brief periods of rest and heavy breathing may have broken up the struggle, but they quickly returned to the scuffle and continued striking and grasping at each other. All night long each man tried to get the advantage. For a time, it seemed like Jacob would prevail. Of course we know that in the end, God decimated Jacob's hip with a simple touch and humbled him into submission. Jacob's response, however, illustrates the attitude the believer must have as he fights against his flesh by God's power. As the dawn rose, God tells Jacob, "Let me go, for the dawn is breaking." Yet, Jacob did not comply. He said, "I will not let you go unless you bless me" (Gen. 32:26.)

Jacob was not holding onto God in victory. He was holding onto Him in utter defeat. Jacob's hip had been completely dislocated and he was unable to walk. God had won the wrestling match. Even though Jacob had prevailed in their physical conflict, God simply touched his hip and the battle was over. But Jacob, completely without strength, refused to give up until God blessed him. Even if it meant his death, Jacob refused to let go of God. This is the attitude we must bring to the fight against our flesh. We are completely dependent upon God. We have no power in ourselves and we cannot love one another like Christ. But we must hold on to Him. We must cling to God's person and refuse to let go until He forms that love within us. This is how our fight is waged, through a desperate dependence on God.

The question before you is simple. Do you really want to love like Jesus? Do you truly desire to love the people that offend you, persecute you, and generally annoy you? Reading a book about loving people won't do. Mentally desiring to love like Jesus is not the issue. Most of the people on the planet say they want to love like Jesus, even if they don't understand what it means. The secular world recognizes that Jesus' teachings on love are valuable and praiseworthy. You may heartily agree that we should love Jesus' bride, but our question hits closer to home when we understand that loving the bride is not a one-time decision. When you ask God to make you more loving, you are asking to be thrown into an epic battle between good and evil. As a disciple of Christ, this war is raging all around you even if you haven't recognized it yet. The war we fight is not like those melodramatic pictures of legendary fables we see in the movies. There is an actual battle between good and evil going on inside Christians. In these fallen earthly bodies, the Spirit of God will continually fight against the evil that remains in our hearts. Although we are justified before God, we are still being transformed daily. The question is, "Do you want this kind of life?" Are you ready to spend the rest of your life at war with yourself? No other kind of life grows in holiness and love.

Unfortunately, the war between the flesh and Spirit isn't as easily recognizable as we would hope...at least until the fighting breaks out. In most wars, the enemies are clearly defined. Each side is discernable because of the uniforms they wear and the definitive battle lines. The war against the flesh is more like the war America fights against terrorism. The enemy doesn't parade around in his colorful uniform, flaunting the fact that he is your enemy. Most of the time, soldiers don't even know they are looking at an enemy until the shooting starts. The flesh has a way of masquerading itself. It makes us think we are justified in not loving others. This is tantamount to making us think we are right to disobey some of Christ's commands.

I have counseled many people who could not bring themselves to forgive a brother or sister in Christ. They just don't see it as a spiritual war. Rather than recognizing the spiritual battle we are fighting, some believers refuse to even take up arms. Instead, we justify our lack of love by any means necessary. Regardless of the circumstances that brought about the hurt, holding hateful grudges is sin...it's as simple as that. But the flesh is very skillful in making us think we are right. I can't count how many times people have said, "You just don't understand what they did to me!" Our sin is cunning and it conceals itself very often by distorting the very principles we claim to hold. Everyone knows sin is wrong. Therefore, when we think someone has sinned against us, it is easy to feel justified in harboring animosity or ill feelings. Rather than recognizing the subtle attack the flesh is mounting against us, we rationalize our hostility because we are "the victim." Even if we truly are the victim, our flesh takes the opportunity to produce sin in us.

A fictional example may help. If Sue spreads a malicious rumor in the church about Betty, Betty feels justified in hating Sue. No doubt, the rumor has hurt Betty's reputation and her testimony. She now spends much of her time doing damage control or wondering what people are thinking. This all started because of something Sue said. Even though Betty did nothing to deserve the gossip, she is suffering terribly under the weight of it. Although this is a fictional example, I'm sure most church members are familiar with stories like this. Usually both parties are somewhat at fault, but, for the sake of argument, let's say Betty did absolutely nothing to cause this predicament. In this moment, as she is suffering because of the sin of another person, there is something inside Betty telling her she is justified in hating Sue. In this scenario, the severity of the offense isn't relevant. By human standards Betty has every right to be offended because of what Sue did. However as a Christian, she probably knows Jesus would have her forgive Sue and let the contempt and hatred go. As a Christian, she would most likely desire to do so, but that nagging bitterness keeps returning day after day. Betty has plenty of "Christian" friends telling her she is justified in her hostility toward Sue. Simply scrolling down Betty's FaceBook feed reveals many comments telling her she has good reason to hold a grudge. But

Scripture doesn't change.

> You have heard that the ancients were told, "You shall not commit murder" and "Whoever commits murder shall be liable to the court." But I say to you that everyone who is angry with his brother shall be guilty before the court; and whoever says to his brother, "You good- for-nothing," shall be guilty before the supreme court; and whoever says, "You fool," shall be guilty enough to go into the fiery hell – Matthew 5:21-22

In that same chapter, Jesus says we are to love our enemies and pray for those who persecute us (v. 44.) He also says we are to turn the other cheek when we are slapped (v. 39.) Jesus even goes as far as saying that if your brother is offended with you, don't even bother bringing your gifts to God. Instead, leave your gift at the altar, go and be reconciled with your brother, and then you may come and present your offering (v. 23-24.) Betty is a true disciple of Christ, so these things weigh heavily on her conscience. She knows what Jesus says to do, but she is bombarded by what her flesh tells her to do. There is a battle going on inside her. Two opposing sides are pulling her in two different directions. Even when Betty decides to completely forgive, every time she sees Sue she has to go through the fight again. Those feelings just keep popping back up.

Of course, this situation is only one of many examples. There are many reasons people are offended with the church. The problem is not the battle. War is happening in believers whether you realize it or not, and we shouldn't make the mistake of telling Betty (or anyone like her) that it is easy to let all the animosity go. It's not easy! That's the point. Forgiveness is a struggle. It's a war. The problem is that Betty doesn't recognize her enemy. She thinks Sue is whom she is fighting. Betty also does not understand why this battle is actually being fought. She just knows she should forgive and it's hard. She doesn't perceive that the voice telling her she deserves retribution is evil and is doing its best to hinder her growth as a Christian.

This war is not about Betty being satisfied with another person's repentance. The war is not about Betty's lost honor...it's about hindering Betty from following Jesus. She is fighting for her relationship with Christ. The flesh rises in us to keep us from being conformed to the image of Christ, but when it attacks, our flesh makes us think it is fighting for our good. Betty thinks she holds a grudge because she has been belittled, when in reality the grudge itself is belittling her in the eyes of the Father. Her flesh tells her she is right in disdaining the person who hurt her, but it is also pulling her further and further into sin. The enemy is fighting to keep her from being like Christ by convincing her that she is fighting to keep her honor and good name. In his second letter to the Corinthians Paul instructs his readers to forgive and comfort a specific individual who has caused them sorrow (2 Cor. 2:7.) Paul's teaching here includes many truths but in verse eleven he tells them that this forgiveness is "so that no advantage would be taken of us by Satan, for we are not ignorant of his schemes" (2 Cor. 2:11.)

When we understand what is actually going on, we begin to get a clear picture of how this war is waged and what we must do to fight back. It is only natural to want good things for ourselves. Even God desires good for His children. But the flesh takes this inclination and turns it upside down so we believe we are seeking our good by sinning against God and others. Will the battle somehow become easy once Betty understands this? Not in the least! But at least she knows where the battle is actually being fought and who her real enemy is. At least she is attacking the right hill rather than flailing around wildly, doing damage wherever she can. When we fail to understand the true nature of this battle, we let the flesh work us up into a frenzy. Once this happens, sin just points us in a direction and turns us loose. We end up fighting against everyone except the true enemy who is attacking.

The Tactics of Our War

We can't really get practical about fighting this war until we get a firm understanding about its nature. If we think the brethren are our enemies rather than our sinful flesh, we will continually fight battles that have no effect in this war. This is all too easy to do. Even now I find myself swept up in battles I have no reason to be fighting. The church folks who are the targets of my frustration are not my real enemy. My real enemy is the sinful flesh driving me. My true enemy is that voice inside my head telling me I am justified in being resentful and carrying a chip on my shoulder. James says this clearly,

> What is the source of quarrels and conflicts among you? Is not the source your pleasures that wage war in your members? You lust and do not have; so you commit murder. You are envious and cannot obtain; so you fight and quarrel. You do not have because you do not ask. James 4:1-2

As someone grounded in the gospel of Christ, I should know that everyone is going to hurt or fail me eventually. Jesus is the only perfect person. Everyone else is a sinner just like me. Everyone else has the same sinful voice in his or her head that I do. So why do I get so hurt when people sin against me? Perhaps I have an overinflated view of what I deserve. If every born again believer is just like me…a sinner saved by grace, then my real enemy is me. Of course, I also have the world and the devil to contend with, but they can only gain a foothold as they dangle their lies in front of me. The only way they can get to me is through my selfish, sinful flesh. Until I am ready to fight my actual enemy, I won't make much progress in the battle to grow in my faith. Once we realize that our enemy is staring at us in the mirror, then we are ready to get practical in fighting the battle to love like Jesus.

What follows are four battle tactics to fight the war against our flesh. These are not the only tactics believers employ, nor do I think that this short book presents everything believers need to know about this subject. What I present here are practical ways to begin cultivating a gospel-centered perspective as we take the fight to our real enemy. Rather than being continually pushed back on our heels trying to recover, we will take the offensive. As I stated in the beginning of this book, I am not a master of loving people. I have a long way to go before I love people like Jesus does, but I have honestly found that these biblical tactics help me take the war to my enemy rather than continually reeling from my failures.

Immerse Yourself in the Gospel

Earlier we talked about preaching the gospel to ourselves. I cannot overemphasize the importance of this practice. In fact, if I had to choose the most important element of the Christian's battle with the flesh, it would be this one. We have already defined the gospel as the incurable sinfulness of man, the unalterable holiness of God, and the satisfaction of God's justice through the death, burial, and resurrection of Jesus Christ. In chapter 4, we talked about preaching the gospel to ourselves in dept so I don't intend to rehash everything said there. However, I do encourage you to go back and re-read that section so you understand the concept.

When our entire worldview is colored with the broad

strokes of the gospel, we see things differently. For example, the good news of salvation starts with understanding that we are devoid of goodness. If we have this truth continually present in our thinking, we won't be shocked when people around us fall short of fulfilling our expectations. In fact, it should no longer be a surprise that people tend to hurt us. That's what sinners do...they sin. In the same way, our own desperate wickedness informs us that we don't really deserve anything good. If every good and perfect gift comes from God (James 1:17), then we must readily admit that we are owed nothing good or perfect. This however does not mean that we have low self-esteem or that we languish in a "woe is me" attitude. If the gospel informs our thinking we also know that we have been given everything good and perfect through Jesus Christ. It is simply by God's grace that we do not suffer any more than we do. The proper question is never, "Why is God letting bad things happen to me?" The more appropriate question in light of the gospel is, "Why does God let good things happen to me?" We already know why people hurt us. They are sinners just like us. The real question we should try to answer is why God lets anything good happen to any of us.

The applications of a gospel-centered worldview in our daily lives are so numerous they could fill a multi-volume work. When we correctly understand the nature of sin and the essence of Jesus' perfecting work, our hearts are beating in concert with God and everything just fits. This doesn't mean the battle is over. On the contrary, this is the first offensive step in fighting the battle. We must clothe ourselves with the gospel armor of God.

The Armor of God described for us in Ephesians 6 has been well explained in many Christian writings and sermons. Each piece plays a role in the daily life of the Christian. But I believe that the one uniting principle of every piece of God's armor is the gospel. The breastplate of righteousness is our perfection in Christ and the outworking of that perfection as we seek to obey Him. Our feet are equipped with the gospel of peace. We take up the shield of faith (faith – through which we are saved by grace.) We put on the helmet of salvation as we wield the sword, which is God's word. All these elements are present in the gospel worldview. Each piece has its own distinct significance but every feature of the complete armor of God corresponds to an aspect of salvation. In other words, the gospel itself is the foundational element in each piece of God's armor. The gospel is how we do battle.

So, when I say we must preach the gospel to ourselves every day, I mean we must continually remind ourselves of our own sinfulness as well as the perfect righteousness which has been given to us. Immersing oneself in the gospel is absolutely necessary to maintain balance in the Christian life. A believer cannot remain vigilant in the struggle against the flesh unless he or she is fed a steady diet of the gospel. Believers must be

WHEN THE SHEEP BITE

continually reminded and refreshed by the realities of sin and forgiveness. The truth of the gospel affects every part of our daily life.

Simply turning on a television and listening to a preacher is not enough. Occasionally dabbling in spiritual or biblical themes as the need arises will never yield the results we desire. The gospel itself is the power of God unto salvation. There is plenty of room in our discipleship for principled instruction and biblical teaching that nudges us toward better behavior and more enjoyment of life, but these things are not the food our soul needs to grow strong. Saturating every area of our life with the realities of sin and salvation is the exercise by which our spiritual muscles grow.

The first thing we must do as we fight to love like Christ is to immerse ourselves in the gospel. Read books about the gospel. Feast on sermons centered on the gospel. Preach the gospel to yourself throughout your day. Meditate deeply on your own sin and the perfection you have in Christ. The gospel of Jesus should be the lens through which we see everything around us. Jesus' death and resurrection must be the centerpiece of our thinking and the determinative feature of our actions and reactions. We must become so engrossed in gospel-centered thinking that when we fail to love like Jesus, we will automatically recognize it as incompatible with our core identity. This doesn't mean we won't have to fight to change our feelings and reactions, but it does mean that our enemy won't be able to sneak up on us anymore.

He won't be able to catch us unaware. Everything we see and think is saturated with the gospel and therefore we can spot the enemy from a mile away.

In the days of Roman generals such as Pompey and Julius Caesar, it was not uncommon for two armies to shadow one another for months. This occurred when one army was moving from location to location while another army "shadowed" their movements as they looked for an opportunity to attack. Many times the armies would line up against each other and although a battle seemed eminent, both generals would stand down and continue moving. Neither army would engage the other if the general felt he was at a disadvantage. Perhaps the weather conditions weren't right or the landscape favored one side or the other. A general would never send his troops into battle unless the positions of the armies and the landscape of the battlefield favored him. Because of this, sometimes armies would go entire seasons following each other and never engaging in battle. Some generals wanted the advantage of the high ground; others needed an open landscape to accommodate cavalry charges. Armies never ran headlong into battle without seeking out whatever advantage was deemed necessary. Fabius Maximus, who is often called "The Delayer," probably saved Rome against Hannibal's Carthaginian army using these tactics.

This is the same way Christians must approach the battles we fight. Our "high ground" is the gospel. We are not ready to address the problems in our life (whether they be behavioral or emotional) until we have firmly planted our feet in the foundation of the gospel. Without this transformational worldview, we are just battling the symptoms of our problem. Unless we immerse our thinking in the gospel of Christ, we are attacking the enemy when he has the advantage. Through the cross, Jesus dealt a deathblow to the forces of darkness (including our own sinful flesh.) But unless we are willing to advance against our enemy from the advantageous ground the gospel offers, we are beaten before the battle starts. You cannot love others in your own strength and from your own heart. The gospel is the only platform from which we can successfully mount that assault. You must immerse yourself in the gospel until every thought, every word, and every emotion is gospel-centered. As believers, locked in the struggle with our flesh, we cannot give up the high ground. We cannot give our enemy the advantage. Make the gospel the focus of your life. Find a fellowship where the gospel is emphasized instead of self-help philosophies. Always keep the forgiveness you have been shown in the front of your mind. Examine the depths of what Jesus did for you and dwell there, content to never leave the foot of the cross.

Stop Feeding Your Enemy

We are fighting a war. The goal of this war is to follow Christ in everything we do, including loving people who don't love us. Our enemy in this war is the person we see in the mirror. Our flesh is active in calling us to sin and tempting us to entertain sinful thoughts. Even though the Holy Spirit within us is sanctifying us daily, the flesh is still present. The Apostle Paul himself said, "I find then the principle that evil is present in me, the one who wants to do good" (Romans 7:21). In chapter 7 of Romans, Paul explores the conflict between what he desires to do as a child of God and what his flesh constantly calls him to do. This pull from opposite directions is real and powerful in every believer. To make matters worse, I often find that when I focus my fight on a particular area of my life, sometimes I end up feeding the very thing I am trying to kill.

If the flesh is our problem, we aren't able to love people in our own strength even if we really want to. Love like that doesn't just happen. No matter how committed you are, feelings of resentment and unforgiveness will always resurface. Our sinful flesh never goes away on its own. The only way we weaken the flesh is by starving it. Paul said it this way, "But put on the Lord Jesus Christ, and make no provision for the flesh in regard to its lusts" (Romans 13:14). "Make no provision," means stop feeding it. Don't give your flesh anything that will feed its lust and cause it to grow strong. Too often believers struggle in one particular area and while they battle that one sin with all their might, they are unknowingly feeding the very flesh that is the source of the problem.

For example, if a man has issues with the sin of anger and his temper often flares out of control, he may do everything he can to stay calm. He may tell himself over and over that he will never let that emotion take hold of him again. He may pray day and night that God will take that anger from him. But the anger itself is not the problem. Anger is a symptom of his problem. The flesh is at the root of the issue. His anger could stem from a fleshly desire to be comfortable or to be in control. When someone threatens his comfort or control, the flesh lashes out again. The man battling anger may read every book available on controlling anger but still not see results. He knows all the right answers. He knows what he is supposed to do and how he should react, but it just never seems to happen that way. He may do well for a while but anger always returns. This same scenario occurs with lust, pride, envy, and every other fleshly desire.

Behind the scenes, the man has focused all his energy toward fighting anger but he is constantly allowing his eyes and ears to feast on things that elevate worldly comfort over a developing relationship with Christ. This worldly consumption need not come in the form of pornography or overtly sexual desires. Whenever he entertains desires that contradict God's word, he is feeding his flesh. Whenever he allows dishonorable affections to enter his mind, he is feeding his flesh. When he does not protect what enters his mind through the gates of his eyes, ears, and thoughts, he is feeding his flesh. Of course, lust is just one of many possible examples. Feeding the flesh doesn't have to come through sexual temptation. The flesh may be fed by any number of means. We feed our flesh when we focus on worldly ambitions or covetous thoughts. We feed our flesh when we engage in the hearing or telling of gossip. It all boils down to a "me-centered" mindset. Whenever we are focused more on our own comforts and desires, we are actively feeding our flesh. And when the flesh is strong and healthy, it manifests itself in all kinds of ways.

The point is that we all have areas of weakness that Christ is busy sanctifying. We know what they are and, because of the Holy Spirit inside of us, we are determined to rid ourselves of them. But these things stem from our flesh. We certainly should engage practical ways to curtail our sin, but as long as we continue feeding the flesh in other areas, we will struggle in every area.

In this book, we are focused on loving people like Jesus. I could give you lots of principles that will help you act in love. I could give you many legitimate practices that will help cultivate love for people in your life. But you will always struggle truly loving people from the heart as long as you continue feeding your flesh in other areas. If your flesh easily overcomes you with bitterness and contempt when you are wronged, it is because you are on a steady diet of worldliness and an overabundance of gratification. The flesh is strong when it is fed daily. In order to weaken our flesh, we must take away what nurtures it. Instead of feeding "self," we must center our lives on feeding our relationship with Christ.

Returning to the analogy of our Roman army may help. In ancient times, the siege was one of Rome's most used tactics to conquer fortified cities. The army would surround the city with barricades and encampments, effectively cutting off the inhabitants' escape. No one could get out and no food or supplies could get in. Unless there was a natural water supply within the city walls, this tactic was extremely effective. The city would basically starve to death and then the army would march in and take control.

One of the most famous sieges in Roman history was Titus' siege against Jerusalem, which ended in A.D. 70 with the city's destruction. When Titus' army arrived at Jerusalem, the Jewish militia groups were extremely fierce and determined. In fact, the historian Josephus tells of many successful Jewish raids on Roman camps. The fighters in Jerusalem were so fierce and the walls of the city so well fortified that Titus could not readily breach them.

So Titus simply surrounded the city and waited. The Romans built ladders, a huge battering ram, and even a makeshift wall around the outside of the city, and while all this was going on, the Jewish people were rapidly running out of food. Conditions in the city became so severe that there were literally mobs of people looting, killing, and foraging for any food available. While the

Roman army sat outside the gate plotting their attack, the Jewish zealot groups wreaked havoc on their own population inside. Josephus even tells of a woman who cooked and ate her own infant rather than starve to death.

Needless to say, when Titus finally broke through the walls of Jerusalem, the Jewish fighters were nowhere near their previous strength. A battle did ensue and the Romans didn't just waltz into the city and make themselves comfortable. They had to fight...and fight they did. But by starving the enemy first, the Jewish ranks were diminished and their level of effectiveness was substantially lower than before.

This is the tactic Paul commands in Romans 13:14. We are at war with our flesh. We are at odds with the part of us that desires worldly comfort and refuses to love others like Christ. Just like Titus did to the city of Jerusalem, we must set up a blockade against anything that would feed our flesh and make it strong. I realize this is probably not what you had in mind when you picked up a book about loving the brethren, but our problem is not simply a lack of love – it is a lack of following the Holy Spirit. We have a "self" problem.

I often tell my students that their eyes, ears, and minds are gateways into the city of their hearts. When we let trash into those gates, we can expect trash to come flowing out in our behavior. When we let ungodliness enter the gate of our city, we should not be surprised that we have so much trouble with godly living. Some people invest their lives in gaining material things to fulfill their happiness. Others can't be satisfied unless they get the perfect job or the perfect spouse and the whole of their lives is spent striving for that goal. Believe it or not, there are even people who work tirelessly at religion because it feeds their self-worth and assurance. We all have a "center" of our lives, a hub around which everything else turns. If this focal point, which receives the lion's share of our love and attention, is anything other than Christ and His gospel, it is feeding our flesh. This doesn't mean we cannot take pleasure in things like a sunset, beautiful music, or time with our family. These things are gifts for us to enjoy from God, but when anything becomes our desperate desire (that for which we hunger and cannot live without) it quickly becomes detrimental to our spiritual relationship with God. It becomes an idol. And idols always feed our flesh.

Our hearts possess the ability to make idols out of anything and sacrificing things to our idol brings us worldly pleasure. If we give up striving for an ever-deepening relationship with Christ for something else, we have sacrificed the true God for a false one. It is entirely possible for us to even feed our flesh by doing good things. Family or affirmation can easily become and idol. If you are one who has not yet identified the area in which your flesh is fed, ask yourself a few simple questions and your idol will readily present itself. These questions are taken from Kyle Idleman's book *God's at War*. The book is centered on the pitfalls of modern idolatry, but I firmly believe that feeding the flesh is linked to idolatry. We feed the flesh when we choose to live for the god of "me" rather than the God of Scripture. Ask yourself these questions and the answers may very well show you where you are feeding your flesh.

1. What consistently disappoints you?
2. What do you complain about most?
3. Where do you make financial sacrifices?
4. What worries you?
5. Where do you feel most comfortable and happy?
6. What makes you angry?
7. What are your dreams and aspirations?[23]

Loving others is not a matter of simply trying harder or doing better. It is about increasingly depending on Christ. If we feed the flesh with worldliness and ungodliness, then the flesh will be an army twice as hard to defeat.

Make sure you understand what I am saying. Of course we know the devastating effects of pornography and licentious living. There is nothing that feeds the flesh faster than these things. But even if these things are not your particular temptation, we cannot simply dismiss the fight because we don't engage in these glaringly lustful activities. We can feed our flesh with anything. When we accept worldviews that are opposed by Scripture or when we place other things before our

---

[23] Kyle Idleman. *Gods At War.* (Grand Rapids: Zondervan, 2013) Ch. 2

relationship to God, we are feeding our inner selfishness. I often find neglecting prayer time because I am too busy, or just needing some "me" time feeds my flesh. This is not to say that leisure time or working hard is bad. These things are also gifts from God. But whenever we place the gift ahead of the gift-giver, we are indulging our own desires and thereby feeding the flesh.

This may sound a little overwhelming at first. You may think I want you to spend the rest of your life walking on eggshells while you look over your shoulder hoping you're not inadvertently feeding your flesh. That isn't the Christian life at all! The point here is simply to show you that there are opportunities for us to feed our flesh at every turn and when we indulge these opportunities, the flesh gets stronger, acting out in ways that are obvious. But instead of targeting the symptoms (i.e. the acting out) we should be targeting the source. We should lay siege to our fleshly mind and refuse to allow anything to enter which is opposed to God's word and Christ's example. When we engage this as a lifestyle, the flesh starves and grows weak. This doesn't mean we won't have to fight, but it means we won't be inadvertently strengthening the enemy we seek to destroy. And finally we will be fighting the right enemy!

Enlist for the Long Haul

Please don't think this battle against your flesh is quickly or easily won. Truthfully, you will be fighting this war until God calls you home. I hope you don't feel cheated having read so far in this book only to find out that the battle you are fighting won't be over until we see Jesus. I really hope you weren't expecting a quick fix by simply following a few rules. There is no effortless way to love the un-loveable and anyone who offers an easy way to sanctify yourself in this life is lying to you. Jesus sanctifies us, often much slower than we would like…and much more painfully.

Enlisting for the long haul is something we must be willing to do. I liken this principle to the myriad of diets I have been on in my life. It seems like I start a new one every few weeks. My problem, which many people are quick to point out, is that I don't really want a lifestyle change. I just want to go on a diet for a few months, lose the weight I need to lose, and then get back to eating what I want. It's easy to be determined about something for a short term, understanding that eventually things will get back to normal. It's not so easy when you realize that I will never be able to eat what I want (as much as I want) again.

Many Christian books give you principles and rules to follow but rarely do they become a lifestyle. Think about how many Christian living books you have read in your life. How many are you still putting into practice on a day-to-day basis? If we truly want to love people like Jesus does, I don't have an easy fix for you. I don't have a six-week program that will turn you into someone that no longer struggles and fights with the flesh. Loving people like Jesus will be a fight until the day you die...that's not very comforting is it? You will fight because your flesh will be a part of you until Christ perfects you in eternity. The longer you engage in this battle, the more readily you will perceive the attacks of the enemy and the more prepared you will be. So it does get easier in that sense. There is growth in loving the brethren. But we will always have a fallen nature as long as we are in the body.

You need to come to grips with that now. You are not signing up for a two-month battle at the end of which you won't have to worry about it anymore. You aren't signing up for a two-year battle either. Committing to loving others when they don't love you is a "rest of your life" battle. There will never be a time when you won't have to take the sword of the Spirit (which is God's word) and slice the head off of your selfishness, pride, and bitterness. Every time your flesh tries to stick its dirty little head up out of the sand, you will have to force him back down by the Spirit and power of Christ. Oddly enough, the battle of the Christian life is similar to a game of spiritual whack-a-mole. As soon as one thing is beat down, another pops up in a different area. Are you willing to undertake such a responsibility? Do you really want to love the people that don't love you? Do you really want to obey Christ? In Luke 14:27-30 Jesus said,

> Whoever does not carry his own cross and come after Me cannot be My disciple. For which one of you, when he wants to build a tower, does not

first sit down and calculate the cost to see if he has enough to complete it? Otherwise, when he has laid a foundation and is not able to finish, all who observe it begin to ridicule him, saying, 'This man began to build and was not able to finish."

Jesus tells those desiring to follow him to bear the cross of death along with him. As Christians, we know the full story of the cross and the resurrection. The symbol of the cross has become a symbol of hope and love for us. However, for those who first heard Jesus speak these words, the cross was nothing more than a symbol of torture and death. It was a humiliating instrument of Roman execution. Jesus had not yet gone to the cross when He spoke these words. Those standing before Jesus certainly would have frequently seen men carrying crosses through the city. The sight of Romans escorting a man carrying his cross meant only one thing. That man was condemned to die.

This is what Jesus calls His disciples to do. We must die to ourselves. In Luke 9:23, Jesus adds the word "daily." He says anyone desiring to be His disciple must deny himself and take up the cross daily. That means every single day for the rest of your life. In Luke 14 (quoted above) Jesus also tells us to count the cost before undertaking this endeavor. No one builds a tower unless he sits down and calculates what it will cost to finish it. It will cost you everything. No longer can the disciple of Jesus live for himself. Believers have enlisted in the army of the Lord and Jesus calls us to a life of war. He calls us to don the Armor of God and go to battle against everything in us that seeks to oppose His rule in our lives. The victory in this war has been won at the cross, but the battle itself won't be over until Jesus receives us unto Himself and presents us blameless before the Father.

Let's face it; loving people who hurt us is hard. It is a monumental battle and it is a battle that we will continuously fight. Even when we think we have put away our grudge, the sight of the person who hurt us brings all those feelings back again. Understand this before you even get started. You are signing up to fight in a war that will rage the rest of your life.

Manage Your Supply Lines

The Middle East has seen its fair share of war. War has been constant there for thousands of years. In the last few decades, America has been involved in the fighting, to one degree or another. For a moment, imagine an average Twenty Year Old from Smalltown, U.S.A. being recruited to fight in the worst area of the Middle East. But instead of first going to boot camp, they drop him in Iraq just like he is. This young man, wearing flip-flops and a Hawaiian shirt, walks around in the heat of battle with no weapons and no training. How long do you think that guy would last? Barely a few minutes I would guess. The thought of some teenybopper nonchalantly strutting through a battlefield is ridiculous. No country would send its children to war in that state. But that's exactly what we are doing in this spiritual war. Many Christians sign up for the battle and simply charge ahead in their own strength, expecting to win a war with no training, no weaponry, and no supply line.

Soldiers who expect to win never go to battle like that! It didn't matter how massive and powerful a Roman army was on the battlefield. If the enemy could cut off their supply lines, eventually the army would fall. Even the most intimidating armies must have food, water, and support. During the second and third Punic wars (Wars between Rome and Carthage) armies used a tactic called "scorched earth." Hannibal, the great general of Carthage, employed this tactic in the second Punic war and the Romans, who ultimately won the Punic wars, used it in the third. A scorched earth policy is when an advancing or retreating army pillages, burns, or uses up every natural resource in their path. The result is that the following army is deprived of supplies.

Examples of this type of warfare are found in numerous historical conflicts. A smaller army, which would easily be defeated in a direct battle, may simply choose to retreat and destroy every resource in its path. The chasing army would then find no food, no water, and no resources to resupply their men. In this way, even a defeated army could inflict heavy casualties on its conqueror. To maintain an army, a general must maintain a constant reliable supply line. General George S. Patton once said, "The officer who doesn't know his communications and supply as well as his tactics is totally useless."

As soldiers in this spiritual war against the flesh, we must always be conscious that we have no supply of power or resources. The raw materials we need for our battle come from the Holy Spirit. Our supply line is our communion and relationship with God. The power of the Spirit is what gives us the tools to overcome the temptations of life. Galatians 5:16 says, "But I say, walk by the Spirit, and you will not carry out the desire of the flesh." The Christian's supply line comes through an intimate fellowship with God and this connection is maintained through spiritual disciplines.

Spiritual disciplines include things like prayer, Bible study, Bible meditation, fasting, worship, and solitude. There are many different types of spiritual disciplines but their purpose is to bring you into intimate communication and fellowship with God. We must remember that the spiritual disciplines are not "good deeds" that earn us spiritual power. Instead, they are simply conduits by which we touch the God who is our power. Donald Whitney explains the disciplines very well saying,

> Think of the Spiritual Disciplines as ways we can place ourselves in the path of God's grace and seek Him much as Bartimaeus and Zacchaeus placed themselves in Jesus' path and sought Him...The Spiritual Disciplines then are also like channels of God's transforming grace. As we

place ourselves in them to seek communion with Christ, His grace flows to us and we are changed.[24]

Unless we stay dependently connected to Christ, there is no victory. In our own strength, we cannot love others as Christ loves them. Fallen humans do not possess the ability to love our enemies from the heart. When unconditional love does present itself in the Christian life, it is always a result of Christ's love flowing through us. The supply line for our army is Jesus Christ working in us by the Holy Spirit. This supply is accessed as we grow in relationship with Him.

The only way any relationship grows is through time and communication. Anyone can start out strong in this battle, determined to overcome any obstacle. But outside of the Spirit, we are all without the strength to complete the task as the seeming endless war rages. I would recommend Whitney's book to anyone seeking a full consideration of the Spiritual Disciplines. However, here I will only comment on two of the disciplines…prayer and Bible study. If you are not in constant communication with God through an established prayer time, don't be surprised when you fail. You are fighting this war without weapons or armor. You are cutting yourself off from your supply line. Grace and strength only come from God. In Ephesians 6, prayer is listed

---

[24] Donald S. Whitney. *Spiritual Disciplines For the Christian Life.* (Colorado Springs, CO: NavPress, 1991) 19.

among the pieces of God's armor and its importance can't be overstated.

Today everything is quick and bite-sized. If we can't express it in 140 characters or less then no one will read it.[25] If we can't get it immediately then it's not worth having. In this rat race of life, our prayer lives often consist of just sending up a quick sentence or two before our meals or as we run off to work. But transforming prayer is not just quickly tipping our hat to God, it is the "quality time" we spend with the one who loves us more than we love ourselves. No marriage would survive if the couple only spent a few minutes a week communicating. Any relationship, no matter what kind of relationship it is, will only grow if time is invested in it. Since our relationship with God is where we draw our strength, it would seem obvious that time is what is needed.

Many believers sincerely desire to develop a powerful prayer life but are unable. If you are like me, you start praying and in a few short minutes your mind starts wandering. My mind floats away toward things that need to be done, what I want to eat later, and just about anything other than prayer. It's a struggle to stay focused. Other people find themselves praying the same old things every day and honestly, it just gets boring. When these obstacles infiltrate our prayer life, we just

---

[25] For you older folks who don't understand the reference, Twitter only allows 140 characters per tweet.

don't see the benefit in praying.

If any of these things are obstacles in your prayer life, I would suggest another book by Donald Whitney called, *Praying the Bible*.[26] His thesis is simple. Believers should take Scripture itself and let it inform our prayers. For example, I might read different psalms daily and pray through each line as I read them. If I am reading Psalm 23, "The Lord is my Shepherd..." I might spend time thanking God for being a shepherd in my life or reflecting on the many ways He is my shepherd. I just pray whatever comes to mind as the Scripture informs my thoughts. In this way, my mind never wanders and I don't just pray the same old things. As long as I can read...I can pray. I simply spend time with my God. Of course my own needs and life events are expressed in my prayers as well,[27] but there is a great power in simply communicating with God through His own inspired word. I may spend time praying, but I must also spend time listening.

In the same way, studying God's word is an absolute necessity in fighting the flesh. More often than not, our experiences and our hearts tell us lies. Our hearts are deceitfully wicked (Jer. 16:9) and given the opportunity, they will gleefully lead us down the road of defeat and

---

[26] Donald S. Whitney. *Praying the Bible*. (Wheaton, IL: Crossway, 2015)

[27] For example, if my heart is hurting for my family, I may spend time asking God to be a shepherd to them before I leave Psalm 23:1.

despair. God's word is the only objective standard by which we can know Him and His will. His word is how we hear His thoughts and attempt to think them after Him. The Sword of the Spirit is the only offensive weapon given in Ephesians' list of God's armor. A soldier cannot expect to be part of an army and be oblivious to his commander's instructions, neither can a Christian obey his master without receiving His commands. But more than that, the Scripture is how we know God. It's how we spend time developing a relationship with God. The Bible is not just telling us about God, it's His own word to us. God has given us the Scripture so that we may know Him, not just know about Him. There is no power in this life without being steeped in the word of God.

We could also briefly speak on fasting, Bible memorization, meditating on Scripture, corporate and private worship, and many other things. But the point is that we cannot fight the battle to love like Jesus in our own strength. We can't love like Him without His love flowing through us and we cannot access the power to love without saturating our lives in the Spiritual Disciplines that draw us into closer relationship with God.

In summary, there are four necessary things believers must do to cultivate their relationship with God and effectively wage war against the flesh. These things can be applied in various ways, but the purpose is to have our hearts changed by being in God's presence.

1. Immerse yourself in the gospel – Saturate your mind and heart with the gospel of Christ. Listen to it, think about it, read about it, talk about it, and share it. Make the gospel the lens through which you see everything.

2. Stop Feeding Your Enemies – Recognize the things in your life that strengthen the self-centered, worldly, or lustful heart and remove those provisions your flesh uses against you.

3. Enlist For the Long Haul – Understand that this will always be a battle. The war is only over when you are perfected in Christ's presence.

4. Manage Your Supply Lines - Be aware that you do not possess the strength to wage this war. You must continually place yourself in communion with God so that His power is the agency by which you battle sin. This is done by a lifestyle occupied with the spiritual disciplines (prayer, Bible study, worship, fellowship with the saints, Bible memorization and meditation, etc.)

Conclusion

Before we leave this practical section, please understand that this is not simply a method that brings forth results. Implementing these four ideas does not mean you won't have to struggle anymore. It's not as easy as 2 + 2 = 4. These four fundamentals are intended to deepen our relationship with God, which in turn motivates and empowers us to increasingly conform to Christ's image. It's not about following rules or completing steps. Developing a dependent relationship with the Holy Spirit is not like unlocking the combination to a safe. It's about placing ourselves in the presence of God. In turn, He empowers us to fight against that which seeks to impede our relationship with God. Fighting to love the brethren is not just struggling to "be good." It's battling to grow in our relationship with God.

Chapter 7

Enough is Enough
Loving from afar?

N ow at last we come to the question you have been asking yourself since you started this book. When do I break fellowship with professing believers who are repeatedly hurting me? Another question I am often asked is, "Does forgiving someone mean I have to be friends with him or her?" or "How do I love someone when I don't really like them?" When faced with the command to love all men, many believers choose to love them from a magical place called, "afar." Loving people from afar usually means just ignoring them.

There are definitive passages of Scripture that command us to break fellowship with some professing believers, so we must take them seriously. In 2 Thessalonians 3:14-15 Paul says, "If anyone does not obey our instruction in this letter, take special note of that person and do not associate with him, so that he will be put to shame. Yet do not regard him as an enemy, but admonish him as a brother." So, on one hand we are to reach out to our brothers caught in sin in order to restore them with a spirit of meekness (Gal. 6:1), but there is also a time to break fellowship. Where exactly do we draw the line?

Forgiveness Does Not Equal Reconciliation

Before we talk about crossing that line of no return, we need to make sure we understand an important distinction. We have already heard Jesus command Peter to forgive the one who sins against him seven times in a day. So let's say this scenario is taking place in your life right now. Imagine someone is continually offending you. Maybe you have forgiven this person several times and they simply will not change. The more interaction you have, the more you get hurt. Jesus specifically commanded that we offer a heartfelt forgiveness any and every time someone offends us. He even made it clear that we are to love our worst enemies. But does this mean that being a devoted Christian means presenting yourself as a doormat upon which people may freely wipe their feet?

I think the answer to this question lies in the difference between reconciliation and forgiveness. Jesus' command to forgive is a requirement of the heart.

Forgiving someone means releasing him or her from the debt they owe. It is something we do internally. We have already seen that forgiveness doesn't just mean putting on a smile and pretending everything is all right. True forgiveness is a heart issue. This is something we must grapple with in our own hearts. Christ-like forgiveness is the genuine release of hostility against those who have hurt us. True forgiveness doesn't depend on what the hurtful person does or doesn't do. It is a battle the believer wages within his own heart and mind. This battle to forgive is a grueling conquest the believer fights within his own life. Fighting to forgive involves struggling to lay aside our pride and conceit as we obey the command to, "Do nothing from selfishness or empty conceit, but with humility of mind regard one another as more important than yourselves" (Phil. 2:3.)

As followers of Christ, we should always stand ready to forgive those who hurt us. Having said that, I am also fully aware that forgiveness is much easier to understand than it is to put into practice. It takes no effort to know about forgiveness, but it takes more strength than we possess to actually do it from the heart. We have already discussed the need for the Spirit's power in this, so we should be aware of how this forgiveness is accomplished.

However, forgiveness is not the same thing as reconciliation. Reconciliation happens when a relationship is restored. No matter what the offense, believers can only be truly reconciled when there is genuine repentance as well as forgiveness. In other words, the restoration of relationship requires the action of both parties involved. Every situation is different, so there isn't a general rule which we can universally apply. Most contention between believers is filled with grey areas as both parties have their own portrayal of the events. There are always two sides to every story. Some situations require believers to relentlessly pursue the restoration of the relationship with the one who hurt them, while other situations would prove unhealthy to seek reconciliation. One Christian who is the victim of a gossiping church member may need to actively try to reconcile with that member, while another believer who is continually hurt by a church member's gossip shouldn't leave himself vulnerable to another assault. The simple fact that every circumstance is different necessitates that God's Word and the wise counsel of the local church are essential for navigating these waters. Make no mistake, these situations always hurt and it is never easy to forgive. But knowing this, we cannot allow our feelings (which are usually driven by pain, suffering, and desires for retaliation) to determine our course of action.

The point is this: Forgiveness is up to you. It is something you must do in your heart by the power of God's Spirit. Reconciliation, on the other hand, is the restoration of the relationship. Reconciliation is when the two believers return to the intimate fellowship which first characterized their relationship. The question is,

"How far do I go before enough is enough?"

Attempting Reconciliation

I can already hear my critics. "That explanation is just vague enough to be useless!" At least, that's what I would say. So let me take you down the scriptural path of a hurting believer attempting to restore the relationship with another. For the purpose of this exercise, we will assume that the mistreated believer has already done the heavy lifting of having a heart attitude of forgiveness. What should he do now?

Involve the Brethren

This may come as a shock to you, but not every person who thinks they have been wronged is correct. Sometimes people with the "victim" mindset are just being big babies and need to suck it up. I can't tell you how many times I have wanted to say that to someone sitting in my office. It feels good to finally get it off my chest. But, while we know this is true, there are others who allow people to tap dance on their meekness because they believe Christians shouldn't stand up for themselves. So how do we find a balance?

Scripture tells us to find that balance in the counsel of the local assembly of believers. Matthew 18:15-17 most applicably deals with church discipline and confronting a believer with their sin. To be fair, some believe this passage is not speaking specifically about a Christian sinning against another Christian, but I believe the same principle applies. (see footnote) The text says:

> "If your brother sins, [against you] [28]go and show him his fault in private; if he listens to you, you have won your brother. But if he does not listen to you, take one or two more with you, so that by the mouth of two or three witnesses every fact may be confirmed. If he refuses to listen to them, tell it to the church; and if he refuses to listen even to the church, let him be to you as a Gentile and a tax collector. – Matt. 18:15-17.

Jesus clearly defines the steps Christians should take in the face of a brother's sin. This passage does not give us a license to go "sin hunting" in other people's lives. Instead, Jesus is showing us the proper way to restore believers to a right relationship with God and the Church. When a church member sins against you, the first course of action is to lovingly show him his fault. The key word here is "lovingly." In order to accomplish this, you must spend ample time dealing with your own heart first. We have already seen how easy it is to forgive with the mind while the heart still rages in anger. Simply making up your mind to forgive is never good enough. True forgiveness only comes as God's Spirit works in the

---

[28] Many later manuscripts contain "against you." While the omission of these words may signal a general view of sin is in view rather than a personal offense, Peter responds by asking Jesus how many times he should forgive someone who sins against him. This may signify an overarching principle at work for both personal and general offenses.

heart. For this, we must take time in prayer and reflection of our own sin. When we focus our minds on the gospel, realizing our sin and Christ's forgiveness, we are confronted with the agonizing truth that we are no more deserving of forgiveness than the one who has sinned against us.

Only after our hearts are molded and shaped by the gospel are we ready to truly forgive, and only when we have truly forgiven are we ready to confront those who have hurt us. Every situation is different so there is no need for us to formulate a stenciled method to address an offender. We must simply align our thinking with the gospel and allow the Holy Spirit to prayerfully guide our words. Hopefully, this will take care of the problem. If the Holy Spirit is working in the life of your offender and you present your grievance in Christ's love, most of the time reconciliation will occur. In a perfect world, that is what will happen.

Of course, we all know this isn't a perfect world. If your loving request for reconciliation is rejected, what's next? Jesus tells us to take a few more believers with you and try again. But we need to do this with reverence and trepidation. Remember, if you are just seeking to be proven right in the conflict, you are not following the biblical pattern. You yourself are sinning because you have not yet properly dealt with your own heart. If your purpose is anything other than restoration and reconciliation, you should go back to your prayer room and allow Christ to continue dealing with your heart.

The second time we go to the offender, Jesus instructs us to bring other believers. The Old Testament law required more than one witness for any legal case to be established. Maybe the offender thought you were over sensitive or maybe he or she felt that you were in the wrong! Whatever the case, another party needs to enter into the discussion.

In this way, the sinfulness of the human heart is tempered by God's presence among His people. In other words, while two disputing believers' disagreement may escalate into a full-blown shouting match, another Christian added to the situation brings a balanced opinion. This sounds suspiciously like pop-psychological logic, but Jesus assured His church that when the church is administering discipline and restoration, He would be present with them. In verses 19 – 20 of Matthew 18, Jesus explains why adding more witnesses (and eventually the whole church) will bring a resolution. He says,

> Again I say to you, that if two of you agree on earth about anything that they may ask, it shall be done for them by My Father who is in heaven. For where two or three have gathered together in My name, I am there in their midst.[29] – Matt. 18:19-20.

Finally, if your brother or sister refuses to repent and reconcile, and the witnesses you employed have agreed that the case must be brought to the church, the local

---

[29] This text speaks specifically about the disputes and disciplining of believers by the church – not just their gathering together in worship.

fellowship must administer discipline. Today, church discipline is politically incorrect, but the Bible speaks of excluding people from the fellowship quite regularly. Here are some examples:

Titus 3:10-11 Reject a factious man after a first and second warning, knowing that such a man is perverted and is sinning, being self.

1 Corinthians 5:11 But actually, I wrote to you not to associate with any so- called brother if he is an immoral person, or covetous, or an idolater, or a reviler, or a drunkard, or a swindler—not even to eat with such a one.

2 Thessalonians 3:6 Now we command you, brethren, in the name of our Lord Jesus Christ, that you keep away from every brother who leads an unruly life and not according to the tradition which you received from us.

Romans 16:17 Now I urge you, brethren, keep your eye on those who cause dissensions and hindrances contrary to the teaching which you learned, and turn away from them.

There are many other verses that speak of rebuking those in error and staying away from those who are causing dissension among the fellowship. In all honesty, we must affirm that the lion's share of these verses deal with doctrinal heresy and people who are corrupting the truth of the gospel, but we can extrapolate the same principle when disputes among believers appear. There are times when we simply must distance ourselves from those who have no interest in reconciliation. However, we should never do this lightly. Our hearts are wicked, as we have seen, and it is easy to justify ourselves in giving people the "cold shoulder." It is easy to think we are obeying the command to keep away from the factious believer, but if there is unforgiveness in our hearts as we move forward with the process, we ourselves are disobedient.

Be Led By the Word and the Spirit

I wish there was an overarching concrete answer for every particular situation, but every situation is different. If the church has hurt you somehow, there are too many possible variables and extenuating circumstances for any uninvolved person to give a hard and fast rule. Working through complex counseling issues is like trying to untangle an extension cord. Just when you think you have it almost complete, a new twist or knot appears. No man can write a perfect strategy for untangling an extension cord unless he is right there working with it himself. There are just too many ways it can be twisted. I can't tell you with certainty that you should keep trying to reconcile or that you should keep your distance from the one who has hurt you.

We do, however, have resources that can manage every particular twist in our situation. God has indwelt us with His Spirit and He has inspired sixty-six books of Scripture to tell us how to untangle the knot. The Spirit Himself speaks to our conscience as we navigate situations in our lives. We should never violate our conscience when dealing our brethren. If everything inside us is saying our heart is not right and repentance is necessary, any council that says otherwise is simply wrong. God Himself guides and disciplines His children and we would do well not to struggle against that discipline.

There have been times in my own life when I thought I could justify my actions biblically, but God was still leading me to apologize. I have not always obeyed that leading and I can assure you that it has always cost me something. Being proven right isn't the point. Winning the argument is meaningless. Being reconciled and united in the fellowship of Christ is the goal. When our hearts burn for vindication, we must take extra care to listen to God speak by His Spirit and through His Word in order to quiet our sinful impulses.

Above, I have listed several verses exhorting the believer to distance himself from some people. It would be very easy for me to take one of those verses, apply it to my particular situation, and claim righteousness in doing what my conscience says is sinful. People do it all the time. To avoid becoming off balance, we can't just claim a list of verses that tell us what we want to hear. As Christians, we must feast on a steady diet of Scripture and hear the whole counsel of God. Taken in a personalized context, any verse can be misapplied and used inappropriately. Since our hearts are selfish and wicked, we are prone to do that very thing. Our own thoughts and feelings can't be trusted as the final court of opinion. As followers of Christ, we must do every thing possible to identify and lay aside any personal tradition or emotional desire when applying Scripture. All of us have preconceptions and traditions we bring to the Scripture. The man who believes he has no presuppositions is the man who is most enslaved to them.

Our sinful hearts necessitate that we follow Jesus' instructions to involve the fellowship of believers and listen to our conscience. The Spirit of God speaks through His Church and to the hearts and minds of the believers. Understanding this, we must always err on the side of love. Regardless of whether reconciliation is possible (or advisable), the attitude of the heart should be love. We are commanded to love the brethren and love our enemies. The person who has repeatedly offended you may or may not actually be a Christian. It doesn't matter. The attitude of your heart toward them should be one of love. While there are times when believers are justified in breaking fellowship with others, and there are times when believers are called to administer discipline to those who are unruly, there is never a time when a heart of resentment, bitterness, and unforgiveness is not sinful. This doesn't mean that you and I won't have to struggle against our own hearts at times. We have already established that the Christian life is often a fight against our own flesh. No one is saying that keeping our hearts free of this kind of enmity is easy. We may indeed have to remove ourselves from the company of some people, for both our sakes. But we never have the right to hold malice, spite, envy, or anger against another person.

This is not a battle we can fight on our own. We will always lose if we attempt it. This fight is not against flesh and blood. We are in a war against principalities and powers and wickedness in high places (Eph. 6:12.) The fight to keep our hearts in check can only be waged by the power of the Holy Spirit working through Gods Word, and in the fellowship of the saints. God has not sent us out to battle as lone Christian soldiers standing against our enemy. He has enlisted us in an army. Each believer is responsible for the man or woman next to him. To forsake the resources God has given for fighting the battle is to surrender to our enemy before the first shot is fired.

Today, we live busier lives than we ever have before. It is common to hear things like, "I just don't have time to study God's Word like I should." In the bustling commitments of an average day, most people don't think they can afford to spend quiet time communing with God in prayer. The fellowship of the saints suffers today like never before, as people simply don't invest themselves with other believers. And when the roof starts caving in on our spiritual life, we all cry, "Why is this happening to me?" We wonder in astonishment when sin creeps back into our lives.

God has given us everything we need for life and godliness. He has given us the avenue for our spiritual growth. When we fail to avail ourselves of the means God uses to strengthen and grow His children, it should come as no surprise that we can't love like we ought. If we keep moving down this path, we shouldn't be surprised when we find our love for God also twisting in the breeze. Our call is to be conformed to the image of Jesus Christ as we seek to know Him and make Him known. "Lone Ranger" Christians cannot carry out this call. Believers who refuse to do the heavy lifting in their own hearts cannot carry out this call. The call is for those whose desperate longing is to be who God desires them to be, understanding that this can only develop as we depend more and more on Christ.

Can we love people from afar? Possibly. We probably need to accept the fact that we cannot be best friends with everyone. However, the question we must answer is much deeper. The question is, regardless of the physical distance we keep, "are we really loving the brethren?"

Chapter 8

And All The People Said...

Being in fellowship with other believers is definitely a messy business. We should be well aware of this fact when we put ourselves in harm's way. Eventually, everyone who invests his or her life in other people will feel the sting of sin. Perhaps someone will break your confidence and air your dirty laundry. Maybe you will be the subject of malicious gossip or be shunned by those you seek to help. There are thousands of ways you may be hurt when you put yourself out there. Sometimes people will purposefully injure you and other times well-meaning believers will inadvertently fail you. This is a reality for which you should probably prepare yourself. Loving others is a messy business indeed.

In this book, I have tried to make sure you understand that conflict is inevitable anytime sinners are involved. Even if we go back to the earliest days of the church, we find conflict among its members. Paul and Barnabas came into sharp disagreement when Barnabas decided to take John Mark on their missionary journey. In Acts 15:36-41, Paul and Barnabas separate due to their disagreement about Mark. John Mark had previously deserted Paul and the Apostle was obviously not ready to trust Mark again.

Likewise, all the Apostles address conflicts in the churches to whom they wrote. Paul addressed many factions that had cropped up in the Corinthian church. The people in Corinth were quarreling about who they perceived the proper leadership to be. Some wanted to follow Paul while others followed Apollos, and still others supported Peter. Paul had to correct these conflicts among them.

There was also internal strife in the church at Jerusalem. James, the leader of that congregation, wrote, "What is the source of quarrels and conflicts among you? Is not the source your pleasures that wage war in your members?" (James 4:1-2.) It would be foolish for us to think that the church is now free from potential quarrels when it has never historically been so.

Sin, conflict, and pain will be realities until the final redemption of creation. However, we cannot say, "that's just the way it is" and leave it at that. If we take all mankind's evil into consideration, it certainly seems easier just to "check out" and remove ourselves from investing in other believers. People do this all the time. Many believers attend worship services and are listed on a church role but refuse to risk being hurt by entrusting themselves to others. To be honest, when we look at the realities of sin and the inevitability of conflict where sinners are concerned, it seems like a good idea to remain aloof from other people. It sure would make life much easier.

Although we have spent considerable time looking at the negative side of church life, I cannot close this work without looking at the blessings and benefits of fellowshipping with the saints. If we concluded our study before examining the advantages and comforts of church life, we would only be telling half the story. Yes...there is great potential for emotional injury in the church, but there are also irrefutable joys and blessings when we invest in God's people. In keeping with the pattern established in this book, I don't plan to be exhaustive in listing the benefits of church fellowship. Neither will I list the social or economic benefits of fellowship that are also true of secular organizations. While there are certainly social benefits, the body of Christ is not an organization. It is a living organism.

However, I don't want to finish this discussion by leaving the impression that loving the brethren is nothing more than drudgery to which we must obey. Nothing could be further from the truth! The fellowship of the saints is an indispensible part of the Christian life and it is one of the greatest blessings God has given. So before we end our examination, let us think about the glorious benefits of fellowship and membership within a local body of believers.

To Fulfill Our Obedience to Christ

Before we look at some of the benefits of church fellowship, we can't skip over the fact that membership in a local body is commanded in Scripture and it is the pattern of the New Testament church. As Christians, this should be enough to mandate membership in a local church.[30] Disciples of Jesus pattern their lives after His word. That being said, the blessings of fellowship are not listed here just to show you how happy you can be. The benefits of the church are not enticements to lure you into doing what Jesus has commanded. We are not saying believers need to be part of the local church just so they can reap blessings and be content. God has commanded it and that settles the question. But we must not fall into the other extreme either. We cannot discount the fact that the church is a means of grace by which

---

[30] Throughout this section, I will use the words "membership" and "fellowship" interchangeably. I see no distinction between the two terms. However, membership does not necessarily mean signing a card or transferring a letter of intent. Membership and fellowship both flow from investing one's life in a local body, whether your name appears on a roll or not. As long as the fellowship recognizes that your life is invested with them, you are a member of a local church.

Christ blesses His people. So, before we dive into the benefits of membership, we must examine the Scripture's testimony of the necessity of investing in the fellowship.

The Biblical Case for Membership

First let me say that membership is being committed and invested in a local congregation. Membership doesn't necessarily include signing a card or placing one's name on a role, although that is the modern norm. Many people's names appear on church rolls that are not members of the church. When there is no demonstrable commitment to the body, there is no membership or fellowship with the bride. On the other hand, there are others who are not on any church list but are thoroughly committed to the local body. Membership is not defined by "signing up." Membership is a lifestyle of responsibility to a particular fellowship of believers.

Christ's church became a living organism, indwelt by God's Spirit in the early chapters of Acts. But even in Acts, as the church was being miraculously formed, we see the Lord adding members to the church. Acts 2:41 and 4:4 record that thousands were being added to the church. In fact, Acts gives us a specific numbering of those added. Three thousand were added after Peter's Pentecost sermon, and the number of believers was counted as five thousand a few days later (Acts 4:4). This "adding" is not just individuals being added to the invisible worldwide body of Christ (although it certainly

WHEN THE SHEEP BITE

includes this.) There is ample evidence in Acts that membership and fellowship were part of the church from the earliest days. Of course, there were no membership cards or church rolls like we have today. Nor were there any established church buildings, but there is a clear foundation for the institution of definite communion with a local community of believers.

Acts 6 records a dispute between two types of Christians. The Hellenistic Jews were upset that their widows were not being treated to the same provisions as the native Hebrew widows. Their grievance is brought before the Apostles, which led to the establishment of the first seven "deacons." Acts 6:2-3 is very interesting in this regard. The text says,

> So the twelve summoned the congregation of the disciples and said, "It is not desirable for us to neglect the word of God in order to serve tables. Therefore, brethren, *select from among you* seven men of good reputation, full of the Spirit and of wisdom, whom we may put in charge of this task. (italics added)

When we read this text, some major questions arise. Who is the "congregation?"[31] Who are these people, and why do they get to vote for the deacons? Could anyone just walk in off the street and vote? If not, then membership and fellowship were essential elements of

---

[31] The Greek word πληθος means multitude, crowd, or assembly.

the New Testament church. When the apostles told them to chose men "from among you," from what body were they to be selected? It is obvious that they were to be selected from the community of Hellenistic Jews. This is why the names of the men were Greek rather than Hebrew (See Acts 6:5.) Already we see the apostles commanding a particular community of believers to choose particular servants from among their own congregation. This fact requires an actual responsibility of membership among the assembly.

Toward the end of the book of Acts, Paul calls together the elders of the Ephesian church. The fact that these elders were known and held an office implies a distinct membership, but more importantly, the fact that Paul was confident his message to the elders would be disseminated to the entire congregation in Ephesus suggests that these elders knew who their members were. The Apostle Peter corroborates this premise when he takes for granted that the shepherds (i.e. elders) of God's people are intimately acquainted with those who are under their care (1 Peter 5:2.) How could they know who is under their care if there is no definite membership?

Likewise, the writer of Hebrews commands believers to obey their leaders because these leaders will give an account to God for their labors. The writer says, " Obey your leaders and submit to them, for they keep watch over your souls as those who will give an account. Let them do this with joy and not with grief, for this would be unprofitable for you" (Hebrews 13:17.) How can leaders give an account unless they know whom they have charge over? Also, how can believers obey their leaders without specifically placing themselves under the care of those leaders in a particular congregation?

Paul also commands Timothy to both help the widows in his congregation and to command widows with relatives to return to their families rather than to accept aid from the church. This would be absolutely impossible for Timothy if there were no semblance of church membership. How could Timothy possibly know which widows had family and which didn't unless they were active participants in his congregation? Also, how could he keep an accurate list of widows in need of help if there is no church fellowship? Who would the help come from without a committed church body?

The New Testament epistles also point to a definitive church membership. The vast majority of Paul's letters were written to specific bodies in different cities and regions. The existence of these letters themselves assumes that those receiving the letters were members of these bodies. In fact, the overwhelming majority of promises made in these scriptures are to a plural "you." For example, many believers claim God's promise in Philippians 4:19, which says, "And my God will supply all your needs according to His riches in glory in Christ Jesus." What many people fail to understand is that the "your needs" which God promises to supply here is plural not singular. Paul is speaking to the members of the church at Philippi. Of course this doesn't mean there is no application to the individual believer, but it is assumed that the believer is part of the local body. The individual in Philippi who has no desire to commune and fellowship with the brethren in that church would have no right to claim Paul's promise.

In another example, the commands in Ephesians to put on the full armor of God are made in the plural. The Spirit here speaks of an army of warriors dressed in God's armor, not a lone Christian trying to wage war by himself. The promises of the New Testament to specific churches explicitly point toward fellowship with the local church. Some may object to this line of reasoning but there is no other way these texts can be understood. Invested fellowship with a local body is assumed throughout the New Testament. To believe otherwise demonstrates a lack of consistency.

Finally, the New Testament is replete with commands for church discipline. Although church discipline is not a very popular subject and many churches no longer practice this kind of discipline, there is no doubt that it is a New Testament reality. "The church is obligated to discipline its wayward members, for this is commanded by the Lord (Matt. 18:15-22) and the apostle Paul (1 Cor. 5:1-13; 2 Thess. 3:6, 14-15)."[32] Yet, without a precise church membership, how is church discipline even possible? Why would an un-invested

---

[32] Floyd H. Barackman. *Practical Christian Theology: Examining the Great Doctrines of the Faith.* (Grand Rapids, MI: Kregel Publications, 2001) 431.

church hopper care if a particular church desires to discipline him or her?

Even if we lay aside all this evidence from the New Testament, we have a direct command from the writer of Hebrews not to forsake the assembling of ourselves together in Hebrews 10:24-25. The text reads, "and let us consider how to stimulate one another to love and good deeds, *not forsaking our own assembling together*, as is the habit of some, but encouraging one another; and all the more as you see the day drawing near." Here we see that the Holy Spirit already denounces the "habit" of some to forsake the assembly of believers. Not only this, but verse 24 admonishes believers to determinately consider how he might stimulate others to love and good works. We are not just to attend an assembly; we are to be intentional in our edifying of one another in that assembly. In fact, we are to assemble more and more as we see the day approaching.

There are also many "one another" commands in Scripture which cannot be fulfilled unless the believer is intimately involved in the local church. For example, the Bible tells believers to "love one another" on multiple occasions.[33] These commands are always in the present tense, which denotes a continuous action in the Greek language. This is not admonishing believers to love other Christians if they happen to see one walking down the

---

[33] At least 6 times in John's epistles, Romans 13:8, and 5 times in John's gospel

street. These commands assume that believers are making a habitual practice of gathering with the believers. There are at least forty other "one another" commands in Scripture which assume church membership. Some of these include being devoted to one another (Romans 12:10), serving one another in love (Galatians 5:13), and speaking to one another in psalms, hymns, and spiritual songs (Ephesians 5:19). An exhaustive list of these "one another" commands would be enormous.

It should suffice to say that the writers of the New Testament took for granted that believers would be active, invested members in a local congregation as they habitually lived out these commands. Indeed, Paul spoke of the local congregation as the "church of the living God, the pillar and support of the truth" (1 Timothy 3:15). In this text, Paul was speaking of Timothy's local fellowship not the invisible worldwide church. He longed to visit this congregation which he called the pillar and support of the truth.

The first and most important reason for communion and fellowship with a local church is because Christ commands it, and Scriptural promises assume it. It's as simple as that. No further explanation is necessary.

To Grow Spiritually

Regardless of what many teachers claim, there is no spiritual growth apart from the fellowship of the saints.

The Spirit of God produces discernable fruit in the lives of believers and that fruit grows as Christians mature in Christ. But the only way the fruits of the Spirit can grow is through interaction with other believers. In an earlier chapter, we saw how the fruits of the Spirit grow as they are tested. Patience grows as our patience is tested. Longsuffering, love, gentleness, and self-control must be stretched to their limit before they can grow. Therefore, it follows that a lifestyle of fellowship with the brethren is necessary for these fruits to increase in the believer's life. We grow as we come to grips with our shortcomings. We produce fruit when we recognize our need to become more like Christ. Usually this realization comes when we are faced with our inadequacy. Believers have to trust in the Spirit of God to mold them into His image. If you decide to remove yourself from the fellowship of the saints and devote yourself to Bible study and prayer, you will definitely grow in your understanding of God and His word. You will also increasingly realize the magnitude of your remaining sin and God's holiness. But until you start putting those spiritual fruits into practice among the brethren, you will never grow in practical holiness, forgiveness, and the outward expression of the grace you have received. Fellowship and interaction with the body is the means by which the Spirit develops those fruits in our lives.

Proverbs 27:17 says, "Iron sharpens iron, so one man sharpens another." This principle permeates both the Old and New Testament. Of course iron cannot sharpen iron unless the two pieces of metal are whacked together. This figurative clashing of iron is rarely pleasant in our lives, but when believers are forced to biblically resolve a conflict, they are truly sharpening one another. But conflict is not the only avenue of spiritual growth in the fellowship of believers. Investing oneself in a local fellowship provides ministry opportunities, corporate worship settings, and focused teaching of God's word. Some may see these as unnecessary in our modern day due to the availability of television ministries and biblical resources permeating social media. Thinking this way is a huge mistake.

Getting our spiritual instruction from the television may provide a measure of emotional safety for believers because there is no need to put one's heart in harm's way. It is much easier to sit in the privacy of our homes enjoying anonymity rather than being forced into social situations that demand our love and attention. But true biblical fellowship and anonymity are mutually exclusive. They cannot exist together. Being a member of Christ's body necessitates engaging and ministering to the other members. An individual cannot be in fellowship with the body by sitting at home watching church services on television. Even if the televised preacher teaches right doctrine from a faithful interpretation of Scripture, fellowship in its biblical form cannot exist without a life investment within a real congregation. Anonymity may provide emotional safety but it is a roadblock to fellowship and spiritual growth.

God is present with His people when they come together in His name, corporately worshipping Him, and edifying one another. This doesn't mean God's presence is absent from the solitary believer praying in secret, but Scripture is emphatic about Christ Himself being in the midst of believers as they gather in His name. The Spirit also uses the life experiences of others to minister to us as we gather together. We will talk more about this under the section about edifying the body but we should at least mention the fact that God uses the exhortations, mercies, and rebukes of other believers to guide our spiritual formation.

We must admit that unless there is an outlet for the exercise of our spiritual fruits, there will never be any growth in those fruits. Without the training of our ministry among the brethren, our spiritual lives will grow stagnant. So many people experience a plateau of dryness in their spiritual lives and don't understand the cause. When believers are faced with these spiritually dry spells, they tend to pull themselves back from the fellowship of believers and, rather than alleviating this condition, it exacerbates it.

A perfect analogy of this concept is found in the Dead Sea. The Dead Sea is a body of water bordering Jordan, Israel, and Palestine. Also called the Salt Sea, this body of water supports no life whatsoever. No plant or animal can survive in this sea because of the unusually high salt content. Most people are aware that this body of water cannot sustain life because of the salt it contains, but few understand why there is so much salt in the Dead Sea. The reason for the Sea's abundance of salt is very instructive for the believer who withdraws himself from the fellowship of the saints. The Jordan River and a few smaller canals empty into the Dead Sea, but unlike every other body of water on the planet, there is no outlet for water to escape. Once water comes into the Dead Sea that is where it stays. Evaporation is the only way water leaves the Dead Sea. Of course, when water evaporates, the salt in the water remains, which adds to the salt content of the standing water. Nothing can grow in the Dead Sea because there is no outlet for water to be circulated through it. In other seas and lakes, salt water enters at one point and exits by another point. There is always a circulation of the salt water. Any water entering the Dead Sea is trapped there and has no outlet. This is the same thing we see in believers. It is very possible to engage one's life in Bible study and listen intensely to true sermons. However, if there is no outlet for these truths to be put into practice, there is no growth in the spiritual life. Implementation of formative scriptural realities and prayerful insights is necessary for those truths to manifest themselves in spiritual growth. If there is no outlet, there is no growth. When believers don't engage in a habitual lifestyle of fellowship and ministry among the brethren, spiritual growth can only go so far before it stagnates.

To Edify and To Be Edified

The local congregation has a responsibility to the members that comprise the body. As members of one another, we are called to edify one another and to provoke one another to love and good works (Hebrews 10:24-25). This is not only a requirement for believers, it is a necessity in our personal lives. Being edified by the body is an area where I find myself falling into sinful viewpoints. In chapter five, we saw Paul's admonition to the Corinthian church in which he likened the congregation to a body. In that text, he said that the eye could never say it doesn't need the less prominent members, and the less prominent parts of the body cannot say they are not needed. The Spirit gives gifts to each believer and every member is necessary for the functioning of the body. Yet, I must admit that sometimes I find myself thinking I don't need the other members. Because of my sinful independence, I would be that member who says, "I don't need people to visit me when I am sick," or "I don't need people to call and tell me they missed me when I am absent." It's easy for me to justify this sinful attitude by saying I don't want to be a burden on others, but in reality, I am justifying my lack of involvement with other people. If I convince myself that I don't need the other members, it is easier for me to assert that those other members shouldn't be such babies when they call for my help.

At one time in our church, three different Sunday school classes met simultaneously in the large sanctuary because we lacked classroom space. One Sunday, as I walked through the sanctuary, I noticed a woman sitting in the middle of the room by herself. Three Sunday school classes were meeting in the corners of the room and she was not involved with any of them. In addition to this, we had many other classes meeting throughout the campus which she could have attended. We have an assortment of different kinds of classes based on age groups, gender, and lesson content. There was definitely a class that would have suited her. After making sure her solitude wasn't due to some crisis or burden she was enduring, I explained to her the various classes of which she would greatly benefit. She looked me straight in the eye and said, "I don't need any Sunday School. I am fine by myself." Rather than go into a long theological discussion about the necessity of fellowship for spiritual growth, I simply said, "But that is how we keep up with people when they are sick or in need. Your Sunday school class will be the people ministering to you and visiting you if you are ever in the hospital." To this she replied, "I don't need anyone to visit me. I'm fine all by myself."

I am not the Sunday school sheriff so I left her there, content that I had offered to involve her in our fellowship. Just a few short months later, guess who spent a few days in the hospital? You guessed it. And more than this, guess who complained afterward that no one from "that church" even came to visit me while I was absent?

I can't be too hard on her because I think the same way sometimes. I am definitely not a needy person and I do enjoy my privacy. However, fellowship and edification isn't just about whether I need someone to bring me a casserole or visit me in the hospital. It is about allowing the brethren to exercise the fruits of the Spirit to me! It may sound noble to say, "I don't need anyone ministering to me," but it is actually sinful pride that drives this mindset. And I don't care who you are or what you say, it stings when no one from your church family bothers to call or stop by when you are going through a difficult time. We are called to edify one another. In fact, we are commanded to do so. The Apostle Paul tells us,

> Do nothing from selfishness or empty conceit, but with humility of mind regard one another as more important than yourselves; do not merely look out for your own personal interests, but also for the interests of others. – Philippians 2:3-4

As members of the body we are not just to treat others like we want to be treated. Rather, we are to regard one another as more important than ourselves. We are to rejoice with those who rejoice and mourn with those who mourn (Romans 12:15.) We are called to carry one another's burdens as we live in fellowship with each other. Our responsibility is not just to minister to the body. We must also humble ourselves and allow others to aid us with our burdens.

Like many people, I find it much harder to let others help me with my burdens than helping others with theirs. Even if you don't think you need help bearing your burden, you are part of a body and that body thrives on sharing in your life. Earlier we saw that, especially when we are mistreated, we need the fellowship of the saints to grow in the fruit of the Spirit (patience, gentleness, etc.) We must also realize that letting our brothers and sisters inside our emotional walls in order to bear our burdens not only edifies us, it grows the other believers as well. Christians are called to use their gifts and talents in the local body, but we are also called to allow others to use their gifts.

Today, we are becoming more and more independent. It has become common for people to say they are "spiritual" rather than religious. As far as clichéd platitudes go, that always sounds pretty good. But when people claim spirituality without being part of a local body, they usually mean their relationship with God is singularly private. Rather than meeting with a group of believers and sharing life with them, it is commonplace to find people refusing to invest themselves with others while claiming to follow the Messiah who commanded them to do exactly the opposite. We personally benefit from investing ourselves in the brethren, but we often don't realize that we do damage to the body when we refuse to fellowship.

One of the most important things we can understand in our spiritual lives is that deciding to invest in, or abstain from membership in a local body is not a neutral choice. In other words, when making the decision whether or not to place ourselves in fellowship with the local church, we are deciding whether we will aid Christ in the world or hinder Him. That may seem a bit melodramatic but that statement is absolutely true. Believer, you are a part of the body. Perhaps you are an eye, a hand, or a foot. Whatever role Christ has given you to perform, it is an integral part in the edification of the church and the ministry of the Spirit in the world. When you invest yourself fully in the local body, you decide to be part of the building of Christ's kingdom in the world. Of course, you must independently testify about Christ, be a witness in the world, and love those in your circle of influence, but you cannot perform Christ's mission to His people without being part of them. Jesus loves His bride and they are living stones being built into a spiritual house. You and I are either part of the building of that perfect bride, or we are part of its wrecking crew. There is no middle ground. We are either caring for Jesus' bride or we are neglecting her. We are either strengthening Christ's church or we are destroying her.

Earlier, we saw an analogy regarding a man departing on a journey and entrusting his neighbor with the care and protection of his wife. Seeing that each member of the body is charged with edifying one another and making disciples until our Lord returns, the analogy fits perfectly here as well. Will the man be pleased with the neighbor who neglected his responsibility to care for his wife? More likely, the man would seek vengeance against the neighbor for not fulfilling his promise. Likewise, I can't imagine Jesus saying, "Well done my good and faithful servant," to those who neglect His people.

In order to fully comprehend the importance of investing ourselves in the lives of fellow believers, let us hear Paul's words in Galatians 6. In the fifth chapter of Galatians, Paul demonstrated the importance of "walking in the Spirit" and he illustrated the fruit which the Holy Spirit produces in the believer's life. We have already documented the fact that these spiritual fruits cannot grow unless negative forces oppose them. In other words, you cannot grow in patience unless someone comes along and tests the limits of your patience.

As he continues writing to the Galatians in chapter 6, he shows the reader some practical applications of walking in the Spirit. Galatians chapter six is extremely important to the edification of the believer and the church body. The exhortations Paul gives here directly tie into his teaching on the fruit of the Spirit.

Paul begins Galatians 6 saying, "Brethren, even if anyone is caught in any trespass, you who are spiritual, restore such a one in a spirit of gentleness; each one looking to yourself, so that you too will not be tempted" (Gal. 6:1). Paul is clearly referencing his discussion on walking in the Spirit by saying those believers who are "spiritual" should restore the brother who has been caught in a trespass. The action of restoring the brother is an integral part of edifying the body, but it is also necessary for the "spiritual" believer to be instructed and edified. Notice Paul says the one who is spiritual (i.e. walking in the Spirit) should restore the fallen brother in a "spirit of gentleness." Gentleness here is the same word Paul uses to describe one of the fruits of the Spirit in chapter five. The believer is to exercise this fruit of the Spirit by building up the fallen brother with this attitude. Rebuilding this brother with the spirit of gentleness is important because we all should be aware that it is easy for we ourselves to fall into a trespass. Paul says we should restore this brother "each one looking to yourself, so that you too will not be tempted."

Paul's statement here shows us that the fruit of the Spirit is to be used in the body to edify one another and for "those who are spiritual" to grow in the understanding of their own frailty. But Paul continues. Galatians 6:2-3 reads, "Bear one another's burdens, and thereby fulfill the law of Christ. For if anyone thinks he is something when he is nothing, he deceives himself."

Not only are believers to restore the fallen brother, but we are also commanded to bear one another's burdens. This is a continuous habitual practice in the believer's life. Bearing one another's burdens is not a one-time event. Paul is exhorting the Galatians to be involved in a lifestyle of bearing the burdens of their brethren. More importantly notice what Paul says. Bearing one another's burdens fulfills the law of Christ. What is this law of Christ? Earlier in the book of Galatians, Paul said that the whole law is fulfilled in a single word...love. When believers love their neighbor as themselves, they will automatically fulfill the law of God. Jesus also said that all the law and the prophets hang on two commands. Love the Lord with all your heart, mind, soul, and strength – and love your neighbor as yourself. The conclusion Paul draws here cannot be missed. If you ask the question, "What does it mean to love the brethren?" The answer is simply, "Bear one another's burdens." This fulfills the law of Christ. Therefore, if we make the question more personal and say, "Am I truly loving the brethren?" The proper question to ask will be, "Am I bearing their burdens with them?"

But there is still another aspect to Paul's teaching here. Investing yourself in a local fellowship is not just about you helping all those poor people who need you. Fellowship with brethren is about you receiving what you need to grow as well. If you are like me, this doesn't really jump out as a necessity. I have always been a solitary and independent person. I would be the person who says, "I'm fine. I don't really need anyone to help me bear my burden." That sounds like strength doesn't it? I may even be humble about it and say, "I don't want to bother anyone else with my problems." But that is not how the New Testament describes this self-sufficiency. Thinking I don't need the brethren to help bear my burdens is prideful...plain and simple. It is sin. Paul shows this to us clearly.

Notice the three letter word that connects verse two and three in Galatians chapter six. The word is "For." Paul says, "Bear one another's burdens, and thereby fulfill the law of Christ...FOR...if anyone thinks he is something when he is nothing, he deceives himself." The bearing of burdens is reciprocal. It goes both ways. Believers in fellowship together are to fulfill the law of Christ by bearing one another's burdens. That means I help bear the burden of others, but I also allow others to help bear my burdens. Here we can see other fruits of the Spirit being grown and cultivated. Especially for someone like me, allowing others to help with my burdens takes humility and meekness. It means I have to lay aside my sinful pride and recognize that I can't live the Christian life on my own. Paul says this because we all have a tendency to think of ourselves more highly than we ought.

Particularly when we are involved in restoring a believer who has been caught in a trespass, we tend to see ourselves as more spiritual or more obedient to Christ than they. It is easy to look at someone struggling with a burden and think they are somehow less devoted to Christ than we are. For this reason Paul continues in Galatians 6:4 saying, "But each one must examine his own work, and then he will have reason for boasting in regard to himself alone, and not in regard to another."

When bearing one another's burdens, we cannot fall

into the trap of comparing ourselves to other people. Sinful pride always sees the best in ourselves and the worst in others. If I am the one helping a fallen believer and bearing his burden, it is easy for me to compare myself to him and say, "Wow, I am doing pretty good." Paul urges us not to do this. We must examine our own lives compared to God's holy standard rather than comparing ourselves to other people. When we see ourselves against the backdrop of God's perfect holiness, we will fully understand that we are not self-sufficient. We are not strong at all and we desperately need others to help bear our burdens.

Paul says that we must look at our own walk and only then will we have grounds for boasting. Of course, he means that if we honestly look at our hearts before God's perfection and measure our work by Him, we won't be boasting at all. At the end of Galatians, Paul himself says that he boasts only in the cross of Christ and nothing else. If we honestly look at our work, we will quickly learn to develop the fruit of meekness. But he admonishes us to never compare our work by the work of another individual and think that gives us the right to boast.

Because of a misconception in Galatians six, I feel the need to explain verse five in this section. Galatians 6:5 reads, "For each one will bear his own load." This statement seems to contradict what Paul said three verses earlier when he exhorted the believers to bear one another's burdens and so fulfill the law of Christ. Now, it seems he is saying everyone must bear their own burden. However, there are two different words used in Greek here. When Paul says believers must bear one another's burdens, he is speaking of the burdens of life as the Holy Spirit sanctifies us and purges our sin. Paul refers to aiding believers in the trials and travails of living in this fallen world. Then he tells the believer who provides aid not to judge himself by comparing his work to others who may have slipped. Instead he is to judge himself by God's standard because when each believer stands before the judge of all the earth, no one will be there to help bear his load. As my pastor often says, "Every bucket will sit on its own bottom."

Following this section, Paul goes into great detail to show us that men will always reap what they sow. If we sow to the flesh, we will reap corruption. Yet, if we sow to the Spirit, we will reap everlasting life. If you take chapter five and six together, you can easily see what Paul intends to say. The Spirit produces fruit in the lives of believers and that fruit is cultivated and grown in the fellowship of the saints. The one bearing another's burden and the one who is being helped both edify each other.

The hurting believer also cannot say he has nothing to offer for the edification of the body. Verse 6 denies this when it says, "Let the one who is taught the word share all good things with the one who teaches." Likewise, the believer who bears another's burden cannot see himself as independent and self-sufficient, not needing the aid of others to grow spiritually. This is sinful pride which is a deed of the flesh rather than a fruit of the Spirit.

Finally, Paul adds to his teaching on the fruit of the Spirit by showing believers how that fruit is cultivated. When believers sow to the flesh, they reap what the flesh produces. Yet, when they sow to the Spirit, the fruit of the Spirit is produced.

It makes no difference if you are one who constantly needs aid bearing your burdens, or if you are one who always aids those in need. You must be part of the local church. Your own spiritual growth depends upon it. You need the church to edify you, even if you think you don't...you most certainly do. If you think you don't, you are proving my point because you have fallen into the exact type of spiritual pride Paul warns us about in Galatians 6. Maybe you know you need the body to help you bear your burdens, but because you realize your weakness, you think you have nothing useful by which the body itself may be edified. Paul also denies this explicitly. Even those who receive help bearing their burden are needed to edify the body.

Make no mistake, Jesus loves His bride and He has placed believers in the body to sustain, protect, and encourage her. Indifference and neglect are not options for members of the body. A hand that rebels against its body is not neutral. It's an enemy. The hand must draw strength and nourishment from the body, and the body must depend on the hand for its strength and nourishment. In the same way, the believer cannot grow without the body and the body cannot grow without the believer.

To Bear Witness to The World

We have already noted that individual believers can and must spread the gospel wherever they go. Personal evangelism is a necessary part of every believer's life. Whether you proclaim the gospel at your job, in your school, or on the street, you are doing what Christ commanded. Yet, simply testifying to the salvation of God is not the entirety of the Great Commission. Jesus told believers to "make disciples" by teaching all the things He commanded (Matt. 28:18-20.) Despite what many think today, disciple making is not just a class which new believers attend. Disciple making requires believers to get intimately involved with each other. It demands an investment of time and emotional energy to walk through life with another person. Disciple making and being discipled is a life-long process which requires more than a single individual. Believers disciple others, who in turn disciple others, and this process continues on and on.

There is, however, a testimony to Christ that no single believer can give. The church stands as a beacon of light testifying to the world that Jesus Christ saves sinners and unites them together in Himself. Believers from all walks of life, with different tastes, cultures, and backgrounds come together at the foot of the cross and are made one through the blood of Christ. Jesus prayed to His Father asking that the believers would be sanctified by the truth. Then he said,

> I do not ask on behalf of these alone, but for those also who believe in Me through their word; that they may all be one; even as You, Father, are in Me and I in You, that they also may be in Us, so that the world may believe that You sent Me (John 17:20-21.)

Notice that Jesus prays for the unity of believers so that the world will believe the Father sent the Son. It just doesn't make sense that people who are so different can come together and be united by a common love and purpose. Their unity doesn't mean they no longer have differences. We have demonstrated throughout this book that believers still have conflicts and struggles, but when the church is operating by the Spirit as the body of Christ, they are salt and light in the world, testifying to the reality of Jesus.

Of course the church doesn't always function as she is intended and as long as the body is made up of sinners, the church will have problems. But the heart changed by the Spirit will always be knit together with other Christians as a testimony to the world. The gates of hell will never prevail against Christ's church (Matt. 16:18.) Jesus Himself said that a significant witness to His power would be the love believers have for one another. "By this all men will know that you are My disciples, if you have love for one another" (John 13:35.)

Although this applies to the invisible worldwide church, it necessarily applies to the local body as well. The congregational unity among believers in a particular community shows forth the power and purpose of Christ to the surrounding area. There is no greater testimony to the gospel than that of incompatible sinners supernaturally transformed to love one another and labor together for the glory of God.

This testimony to the power and glory of Christ has endured through the centuries since Jesus arose from the dead. Even in Paul's day we see churches like the one in Corinth which was beset with sin, disunity, and a host of problems. Throughout time the church has been threatened by a host of enemies and internal issues which may have easily destroyed it. The very same thing exists today. Yet, the church endures. The worldwide church endures and the multitude of local bodies that make up the universal church endure. When a believer invests his or her life in a local fellowship, he joins that testimony by saying Jesus' bride is worth living and dying for. On the other hand, a believer who neglects the body of Christ in his or her community testifies that the bride whom Jesus loves is not that important. This "Christian" proclaims to the world that God's people aren't worth investing in. This, in turn, implies that submission to Christ Himself is a matter of convenience.

If someone who knew nothing about you, was given a video displaying thirty days of your life, would they say that God's people are important to you? They are certainly important to Jesus! What kind of testimony are you giving to the world?

Adding It All Up

The sun rose upon a very strange Monday morning. A donkey strolled out from the makeshift stable into the glaring sunlight. This was no ordinary Monday and this was no ordinary donkey. As the donkey took in the first glimpse of the morning scenery, he said to himself, "Today will be the greatest day ever." Crowds of people were walking up and down the city streets. The city itself buzzed with the excitement and expectation of what lay ahead.

As the donkey meandered his way out into the streets, something was different. No one was paying any attention to him! People walked passed him without even a second glance. Some people were even aggravated because they were forced to walk around him as they hurried to their destinations. "Don't you know who I am?" The donkey said to himself. "Just yesterday all of Jerusalem stood before me gasping in astonishment and shouting "Hosanna" as I entered into the city. Yesterday, no thoroughbred stallion was more prominent than I. Yesterday, the King of the Universe chose to use me for His service." But now, no one cared. Twenty-four hours earlier, the donkey was at the center of history itself. Today, he is just another donkey.

Nothing changed in the donkey between yesterday

and today. The only difference was that yesterday, Jesus used the donkey for His purposes. Surely by now you realize that this donkey was the animal on which Jesus triumphantly entered Jerusalem as the Passover Lamb. How Jesus procured the beast of burden is a well-known story in the gospel narrative. Mark 11:1-3 reads,

> As they approached Jerusalem, at Bethphage and Bethany, near the Mount of Olives, He sent two of His disciples, and said to them, "Go into the village opposite you, and immediately as you enter it, you will find a colt tied there, on which no one yet has ever sat; untie it and bring it here. If anyone says to you, 'Why are you doing this?' you say, 'The Lord has need of it'"; and immediately he will send it back here.

What a glorious thing to hear. The Lord has need of you! It may be a bit disconcerting that I just subtly compared you to a donkey. I must confess that although I have often been called a "jackass," I intended the comparison in the most complimentary way. Jesus, the King of kings, told His disciples that He needed the donkey. This colt would be the vehicle that would carry Him to fulfill Old Testament prophecy and complete the mission of redemption.

The sovereign God will certainly do what He pleases and He needs no help from any creature on the planet. Even so, He has chosen that we, His collective children, would be the vehicles by which a lost world is reached and His bride is strengthened. What an honor and a responsibility! Does this mean that life will always be a bed of roses? Of course not! In fact, we should probably expect difficulty, pain, and heartache. But even in the midst of the trials we will face, we have been commissioned by the King to seek and save that which is lost, and to edify the bride whom our Savior loves.

The Lord has need of you today. He calls you to a mission. He calls you to war. Believers will always fight against their remaining sin and the expression of that sin among those we seek to edify. It will be messy and it will cost us, but service to our King is not without its glorious benefits. Christ has need of you and, like it or not, you have need of Him. If you are born again, you hunger and thirst for righteousness. That appetite is only filled as we develop a relationship with our God and His people. Christ grows the fruit of the Spirit in our lives by confronting us with people who will continually test the limits of that fruit. These conflicts are difficult and painful but they are certainly necessary for our spiritual growth and the life of the church. Yes, Jesus and the bride have need of you, but you certainly also need the fellowship of the saints. As strong and as self-sufficient as you may be, you cannot serve the living God outside of the means He has chosen to minister in the world. Para-church ministries are important and useful but they can never replace the living organism that is the body of Christ.

You need the church and the church needs you. Not only does the local body need your attendance and your financial support, they need you! The church needs you to invest your life in them. There are believers who are hurting and because of the trials you have endured, you are perfectly equipped to help. Not only this, but you need to grow spiritually through fellowship with other believers who have victoriously emerged from circumstances akin to your own. You need them and they need you.

Jesus asks you today, "Believer, do you love me?" No doubt you will look into your heart and say, "Yes Lord, you know that I love you." Christ's reply is singularly focused to you today. "If you love me, then feed my sheep!"

About the Author

Jason Velotta is the Associate Pastor of Christ Church in Brownsville, TN and a Chaplain at Jackson Madison County General Hospital in Jackson, TN. He earned an MDiV, an MABS, and an MM from Temple Baptist Seminary.

Jason has also authored two other books.

Reclaiming Victory: Living in the Gospel demonstrates that salvation itself is the victorious Christian life. Believers need not chase after the latest self-help methods and moralistic principles to reach a higher level of spirituality. Life should never be just a rat race chasing after joy. Being made perfect in Christ is the pinnacle of a relationship with God and the abundant life. *Reclaiming Victory* is a refreshing biblical exposition of Christ's perfect salvation. Believers will find their victorious life right where they left it...at the foot of the cross.

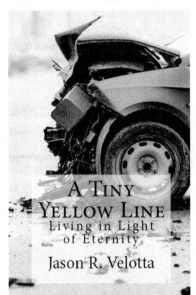

A Tiny Yellow Line: Living in Light of Eternity examines the biblical truth about heaven and hell. So many of Christ's disciples still fear death and the life to come because of popular misconceptions about what eternity will be like. Will we know each other? What kind of body will we have? Will we retain our personalities and identity? These are questions the Bible definitively answers. Understanding this produces a joy and expectation in this life. Believers are called to truly live, not just keep busy until we die.

Jason lives in Brownsville, TN with his wife Dana, and their three children Jacob, Jesse, and Sophie.

He also operates www.jasonvelotta.com which provides free audio and video resources, chapter by chapter mp3 expositions of the Bible, an accessible theology curriculum for Sunday Schools, and a catalog of books, articles, and sermons.

Made in the USA
Middletown, DE
29 December 2020